A Treasury of
Georgia Tales

A Treasury of
Georgia Tales

Webb Garrison

RUTLEDGE HILL PRESS
Nashville, Tennessee 37210

Published in Nashville, Tennessee, by Rutledge Hill Press, Inc., 513
Third Avenue South, Nashville, Tennessee 37210

Typography by ProtoType Graphics, Inc., Nashville, Tennessee

Library of Congress Cataloging-in-Publication Data

Garrison, Webb B.
  A treasury of Georgia tales.

  Includes index.
  1. Georgia—History.   2. Georgia—Biography.
I. Title.
F286.G3   1987   975.8   87–23255
ISBN 0-93495-66-7

Printed in the United States of America
4 5 6 7 8 9 — 94 93 92 91

Thereby Hangs a Tale

Annual conventions of storytellers always include a few bull sessions devoted to asking, What makes a really good tale? No one has a sure-fire formula. But these discussions, plus Shakespeare's famous phrase, "Thereby hangs a tale," suggest a partial answer. A really good tale hangs upon a fairly familiar person or event, but includes unfamiliar details or a surprise twist not widely known.

Georgia tales presented here are aimed at the target of familiarity-plus-novelty. They span the state's 250-plus years of existence and range from the Atlantic Ocean to Alabama, from the Florida state line to Tennessee.

Many of these tales were initially suggested by readers of the *Atlanta Journal-Constitution*. Most were exposed to this wide newspaper audience before being re-written for this collection. These suspense-packed stories constitute "history for the ordinary person," and a few include really great traditions passed orally from generation to generation.

Here's hoping that you enjoy . . . and enjoy . . . and enjoy . . . and maybe get a few real surprises!

—Webb Garrison

Table of Contents

PART ONE:
High Adventure

1

John Wisdom Made Paul Revere Look Like a Sissy

No artist ever sketched his portrait. No nationally famous poet ever sang his praise. As a result, John H. Wisdom is practically unknown.

Yet his trek to save Rome from the Yankees made Paul Revere's midnight ride seem like a pleasant Sunday outing.

Revere's exploit on April 19, 1775, covered nine miles and required two hours. A single horse was enough for the feat.

John Wisdom's ride on May 2, 1863, took him sixty-seven miles during eleven hours. He wore out four horses and one mule and reached his destination on a fifth horse that was barely able to canter.

Wisdom, who once lived in the North Georgia city of Rome, knew it to be of vital importance as a key rail center and also the location of a cannon factory that at one time had employed a thousand men.

Now living in eastern Alabama, Wisdom was out on his mail route when he heard that "a huge bunch of Yankee soldiers are headed straight for Rome." He decided forthwith to beat them to the city and sound the alarm.

Still in the buggy he used for carrying mail, Wisdom dashed off about 3:30 P.M., covering twenty-two miles in a little more than two hours.

Leaving the buggy and his weary horse with the Widow

Hanks, he made five more miles on a lame pony borrowed from her. At the Johnson farm, he got a fresh mount on which he galloped eleven miles to the home of the Reverend Joel Weems.

At Weems's place he got a new horse, but the animal proved to be slow and clumsy. Wisdom had no luck in swapping it for another, though, until within sight of the Georgia line.

Racing through Vann's Valley, his mount stumbled and fell. Wisdom was thrown but had no broken bones. He remounted, rode another twelve miles, and found nothing but a mule. Then he crawled from the mule to mount a worn-out old plow horse for the last leg of his journey.

John Wisdom reached Rome at four minutes before midnight and rode through the streets yelling, "The Yankees are coming! The Yankees are coming!"

Awakened citizens included few males of fighting age; they were far away, in Confederate uniforms. A few boys and old men rounded up squirrel rifles, shotguns, and one old muzzle-loading musket.

A handful of wounded soldiers staggered out of the Rome hospital to take charge of the "home guard." Cotton bales formed breastworks to protect about forty boys and old men. Someone found two rusty old cannon so honeycombed they could not be fired, but they were dragged to the battle line and positioned so from a distance they would seem to pose a threat. By sunrise, six hours after Wisdom's arrival, Rome was as ready for the enemy as she would ever be.

An advance guard of Yankees surveyed Rome's defenses through field glasses in the dim light of dawn on Sunday, May 3. They concluded that their target was protected by the Georgia Home Guard.

Believing themselves to be outnumbered and outgunned, the Yankee patrol returned with word that Rome was too strongly fortified to warrant attack. The Union commander, Colonel A. D. Streight, knew that behind him was a much smaller force of Confederate cavalry under General Nathan

Bedford Forrest. He seemed to be caught in a vise.

Before noon on the day they turned back from Rome, the entire Union force surrendered to Forrest and his cavalry-men. A very small group of Rebels cautiously followed at a safe distance.

In the excitement of the victory, the people of Rome hailed Forrest as their deliverer but paid little attention to John Wis-dom, who rode quietly back to Alabama to continue to de-liver the mail.

2

Perilous Voyage to an Unknown Destination

"Come with me," urged James Oglethorpe to an unemployed cloth maker. "Below Carolina, we shall create an ideal colony. No one will go hungry, and everyone will have work. It is the opportunity of your lifetime; if you pass up this chance, you'll never have another like it!"

The former member of Parliament proved as persuasive conversing with the idle poor of London as he had been in debate. While he had never been to the land that was named in honor of King George II of England, he was supremely confident that, under his leadership, Georgia would become a haven for the homeless and oppressed of Europe.

After recruiting male and female followers, Oglethorpe bargained with ships' captains until he finally engaged the tiny *Ann* for the crossing. However, delay followed delay; and on November 16, 1732, departure was postponed yet another day because the pilot was drunk. Since no member of the party had ever crossed the Atlantic, it did not occur to them that delay put the voyage deeper into the fierce winter season.

To the owners and seamen of the vessel, the passengers were only freight, with the trans-Atlantic voyage charged at four pounds per head. An adult was counted as one head, while children were counted in fractions according to age. Rations for the voyage consisted of salt pork, salt beef, salt

*Georgia's founder,
James Oglethorpe.*

fish, bread, suet, and plums.

Precisely how many persons were aboard, no one knows. A passenger, Peter Gordon, started a detailed journal but gave it up because of seasickness. He recorded that forty-one men, twenty-seven women, and twenty-eight children were housed in the hold. Oglethorpe had a splendid cabin.

Five weeks out of port, with Christmas only a few days away, it seemed an appropriate time to celebrate. A live sheep brought aboard for Oglethorpe's table was slaughtered and roasted over the customary open fire that was the dread of every master of a wooden ship. Along with the mutton, Georgia's founder provided "a quantity of liquor to drink the health of the day."

*Even before the Ann's sails were lost, the tiny ship
wallowed in heavy seas.*

After the evening meal, the passengers who expected to
become Georgians "were diverted with cudgell playing," a
pair of shoes being the prize awarded to the best player in
this form of mock combat. Eventually becoming tired of the
contest that used short, thick sticks as weapons, they turned
to what Peter Gordon called "skimingtons." In this form of
horseplay, someone was ridiculed and thirty-two-year-old
Anna Coles was selected as the butt of their humor. A few
days earlier, she had loudly berated her husband, a cloth-
worker ten years her senior.

When the farce was over, the future colonists went to bed
with happy smiles and full stomachs. Christmas Day, they
told one another, would be even better.

The holiday dawned with squalls and heavy clouds, and
soon the little ship began to pitch and toss wildly. Then a
gust swept away the topsail on the mizzen, or third, mast,

making it difficult for the seamen to handle the vessel. The *Ann* would not be able to continue its speed, and provisions were running low.

The Reverend Henry Herbert, who had gone along as a volunteer chaplain, didn't have to urge fellow passengers to come to the great cabin for prayers, although earlier they had sometimes balked at gathering for worship and a sermon.

December 26 brought even fiercer winds. Before the day was over, the *Ann* lost her big "main top gallant" sail. Never easy to handle, the crippled ship now moved even slower. Tight-faced and grim, James Oglethorpe ordered that the daily allowance of water and beer be reduced by one pint per head.

The sick and frightened passengers crowded on deck for the funeral of nine-month-old James Clark. A terse log kept by merchant Thomas Christie said simply, "Clark's Child was throwd over board & the Ceremony decently performed."

With seas still running so high that the ship lurched continually, food was reduced to salt fish and moldy bread. Suddenly a sailor spotted a clump of seaweed. "Land ahead!" he shouted joyfully.

His cry brought the entire ship's company running, and the battered, seasick, hungry, and frightened passengers bowed their heads as Dr. Herbert gave thanks for having safely arrived at "the end of a voyage during which each of us despaired many times, but which has brought us to our unknown land of promise."

3

Shotgun Totin' Dentist Was Pivotal at the O K Corral

"It's about time. Sure, I'll go along."

According to an eyewitness, that's all John Henry Holliday said in response to police chief Virgil Earp. Hastily, the officer had outlined a plan of action aimed at putting an end to trouble from the Clanton gang.

Born in Griffin in 1851 and reared in Valdosta, Holliday practiced dentistry briefly after winning a degree from a Pennsylvania college in 1872. However, when his persistent cough was diagnosed as a symptom of tuberculosis, he was advised by a doctor to "Hunt a dry climate, maybe in the West. It could give you an extra year to live."

Doc Holliday stopped at Dallas because the railroad ended there, but it took only a few weeks to learn that dentists were not in great demand in the brawling cow town.

So the Georgian, who was blessed with strong and steady hands, decided to put them to work where they'd pay the best dividends, at faro tables. Soon he had won local renown as a top-drawer professional gambler.

That meant he could handle the cards with the best. It also meant he could hold his own against the assorted deadly weapons present at every card game. Many a hustler carried four, or even as many as ten, assorted weapons; Doc decided that, for him, three were enough.

For his visible weapon Holliday carried a six-gun in his

*John Henry ("Doc")
Holliday.*

hip holster. To avoid shooting himself accidentally, he never put more than five cartridges into the weapon. When not in use, the hammer always rested against an empty chamber.

A shoulder holster concealed under his left arm put his second gun within easy reach of his right hand, but the weapon he used with the greatest zest was a sheath knife in his breast pocket. Over and over, it found its mark while the man who had cheated on Doc or had challenged him was reaching for his gun.

Doc knew all the famous men and infamous places of the Wild West. He saved the life of Wyatt Earp three times. He won clemency from the governor of Colorado at the intercession of Bat Masterson. He gambled with Sam Bass and Cole Younger.

Holliday was in Dallas, Austin, Indian Territory, Cheyenne, Denver, and Fort Griffin. He coughed his way through

Leadville, Dodge City, Old Town, Las Vegas, Trail City, and Prescott. His traveling companion, Big Nose Kate, sometimes went by the name of Mrs. Holliday. She had saved his life by burning down a hotel where he was held prisoner. Long ago he had severed all Georgia ties, except for exchanging an occasional letter with a cousin in an Atlanta convent.

In 1880 Doc followed Wyatt Earp to Tombstone, where during the last week of October, 1881, law and order collapsed when a long-standing feud between the Earp brothers and a cowboy clan led by Ike Clanton reached the boiling point.

Soon after breakfast on the 25th, Virgil Earp, a law enforcement officer, banged Clanton over the head with his gun barrel because his enemy had resisted arrest when told he'd violated an ordinance.

Within an hour, Wyatt met the unarmed Clanton ally Tom McLowry in the street. Protected by his badge, Earp slugged McLowry until he dropped, bleeding, into the gutter.

By noon, everyone in Tombstone knew that Ike Clanton had sent for help. They'd meet at the O K Corral, an open air livery stable facing the main street.

Virgil Earp decided not to wait for his foes to make the first move. With his two brothers he started for the O K Corral. Doc Holliday stopped them long enough to learn about their plans. Then he grunted approval and said he was ready to join them.

Half a block from the corral, Doc swapped his cane for Virgil's sawed-off shotgun, which he slipped up the sleeve of his long topcoat.

Nineteen-year-old Billy Clanton had two guns in holsters that swung from his belt. Five other members of the Clanton party had a six-gun each. Two rifles were stashed in saddle boots of horses hitched at strategic points.

Since each of the three Earps and Holliday had one pistol, their only ace in the hole was the concealed shotgun carried by Doc.

Lengthy legal hearings never settled the question of who fired the first shot. Witnesses disagreed about nearly every detail of the fight, except its duration and the sequence of events that brought it to an end.

"It was short, awful short," testified Sheriff John Behan, who didn't have jurisdiction over the town of Tombstone but who had watched intently. Some said three men were killed and three were wounded in, maybe, thirty seconds; others said there weren't fifteen seconds between the first shot and the last.

Hit in the belly by a slug from one of the Earps, Frank McLowry bent double with pain. Billy Clanton took one in his chest. All three of the Earps were wounded by now.

Tom McLowry made a jump for a rifle.

Until then, Doc Holliday hadn't had a clear field of fire, but as Tom reached for the Winchester, Doc tore him apart with both barrels of his shotgun.

Holliday dropped the now-empty gun and pulled out his Colt .45, a fine nickle-plated weapon, with the hammer, as usual, on an empty chamber.

By now most action was in slow motion or had ceased altogether, so it was easy for Frank McLowry to know when Doc had fired four shots and had just one left.

Described as "grinning like a stuffed wolf," McLowry bore down upon the gaunt ex-dentist. McLowry and another member of the Clanton gang fired simultaneously. Both shots missed vital spots.

Wounded in hip and back, Doc lifted his piece slowly. Then he squeezed the trigger, put a bullet through Frank's heart, and ended the Gunfight at the O K Corral.

Frank McLowry was Doc Holliday's thirtieth victim, by most counts. Some say the tally would go much higher if the names of men who'd died around faro tables in one-horse towns were included.

In a desperate bid for a few more months of life, the Georgian went to Glenwood Spring, Colorado. There he drank the stinking sulfur water of the health resort, but grew worse rather than better, dying on November 8, 1887. Had he lived two weeks longer, he would have celebrated his thirty-sixth birthday.

4

Burke County Boy Gained Lasting Fame from a Knife

Until the time of the American Revolution, Georgia had no counties, just two big parishes. Then under the constitution of 1777, the state was divided into eight counties with one of them, Burke, being created largely from land gained from Creek Indians in 1733.

Rezin and Alvina Bowie, who had a cabin in a desolate section of Burke County, barely managed to scratch an existence out of the ground, yet they had ten children to feed and clothe.

One of their boys, James, was just three years old when his folks decided they'd had enough of Burke County. Originally from Maryland, they had come South in search of cheap land, but they decided it wasn't worth even what they paid for it. So they moved westward and were still in Georgia when they reached the Mississippi River.

In 1802 these pioneers settled in Catahoula Parish, Louisiana and were becoming adjusted to living under Spanish rule when Thomas Jefferson engineered the Louisiana Purchase. The Bowies once more were back in the United States.

Twenty-five years after Jefferson's big buy, in September, 1827, Jim Bowie was a principal in the first of many recorded exploits, the stuff of which frontier yarns are spun.

Two leading families of Alexandria, Louisiana, had been

Col. Jim Bowie.

feuding for years, without bloodshed. But on September 19, Montfort Wells and Dr. Thomas H. Maddox decided to settle their differences with dueling pistols.

Meeting on a sandbar in the Mississippi River, across the state line from their homes, they exchanged two shots. Neither man was hit, so they shook hands and called it quits.

Before they could get to their boats, however, their relatives and friends appeared. One pulled a gun; another let go with his deer rifle. Those who survived the ensuing free-for-all counted six dead men on the sandbar and another fifteen wounded.

Jim Bowie, shot early in the fracas, threw away his gun. Then he pulled out an enormous knife. Ground from a blacksmith's file, it measured sixteen inches in length and was complete with a hand guard. Slashing right and left, the enormous blade put a quick end to Major Norris Wright. No one knows how many others died from it or crawled off to bandage their wounds.

Within a matter of weeks, folk on the frontier were talking about the Bowie knife that was as fearful as any gun. Ideal for hand-to-hand combat, it could be thrown hard and accurately because the large handle balanced the blade. Somehow, a Philadelphia cutler acquired a model of it and made copies. One of them went to Sheffield, England, where the Bowie knife soon was being precision made for shipment throughout the Western world.

Years later, militant abolitionist John Brown planned his famous Harper's Ferry raid carefully. In order to arm the slaves he expected to liberate, Brown ordered a thousand Bowie knives. Fastened to six-foot poles, they made the meanest pikes a fellow ever saw.

Fame of the knife has obscured many other facets of Jim's life.

For many people the change in national ownership of the land known as the Louisiana Purchase, resulted in chaos. It was hard to substantiate the validity of titles to property. Yet somehow, Bowie, a man with no legal training and a reputation only as a frontier brawler, managed to gain titles to 119 parcels of land. In 1828 the territorial court of Arkansas validated all 119 deeds.

How he acquired all that land remains an unsolved mystery, as does the question of what he did with the money he got for it.

One story says that Bowie used his profits to buy slaves, then took them to Texas and sold them for a profit of $60,000. Another tale insists that he channeled much of his money into the hands of pirates, with whom he was a silent partner.

Nevertheless, it is certain that Big Jim became bored with the tame life of Louisiana and Arkansas. That is why he went to Texas where he became a colonel of volunteers in the Texans' fight for freedom from Mexico.

Knowing that San Antonio was certain to fall, General Sam Houston sent Colonel Bowie and thirty men there with orders to destroy the one-time Alamo mission that had become a fort so it wouldn't pass into Mexican hands. Bowie disobeyed his commander-in-chief and decided to defend it instead.

To this day Americans "Remember the Alamo" and the story of how at the end of these "thirteen days of glory" Jim Bowie died wielding his enormous knife in the fight for Texas independence.

5

Freedom Fighter James W. Fannin Marched to His Death

"That Georgia boy is gonna get him a passel of Mexicans before this thing is over!"

Volunteers sprawled around a self-appointed sergeant in the new revolutionary army of Texas nodded eager agreement. They'd seen James W. Fannin in action at Gonzales on October 2, 1835. History books call it a skirmish, but it was at Gonzales that the first blood was shed in the Texas war of independence.

Fannin, a freedom fighter who led a company of volunteers, was a crack shot. He picked off Spanish-speaking foes almost as casually as though he had been shooting squirrels back home in Twiggs County, Georgia. Greatly admired by other volunteers, at age thirty-one he had already had seventeen years of experience as a fighter. In 1819 at age fourteen, he won an appointment to West Point, but a quarrel with a fellow student caused him to run away from the military school and return to Georgia. By 1834 he had accumulated a wife, two children, and enough borrowed money to strike out for the land of opportunity—Texas.

Settling at Velasco on the Brazos River, he prospered and by the time some of his fellow Yankees decided to cut the region's ties with Mexico, Fannin owned thirty-six slaves. He kept in touch with relatives back in Georgia and often sent them unusual gifts. Once his half sister received from him two ring-striped pigeons, a box of sea shells, and two guinea pigs.

As a hero because of his action at Gonzales, Fannin advocated taking the war to Mexico's home soil. Governor Sam Houston bitterly opposed this strategy, but he couldn't prevent volunteers from elevating Fannin to the rank of colonel.

When Sam Houston was out of the region, as he often was, Colonel Fannin was the senior officer of the Texas army and in that capacity he got the chance he wanted.

When a force of about 500 volunteers—about half of them from Georgia—arrived, he led them across the San Antonio River to Compano on the south bank.

While Fannin consolidated his position, Mexican General Santa Anna prepared his advance upon the Alamo. He directed General Jose Urrea, commander of his right wing, to crush the Texans, who judiciously withdrew to Fort Goliad. The attack started on February 13, 1836, ten days before Santa Anna reached the Alamo.

Outnumbered and outgunned, Fannin held out as long as he could, then retreated with the hope of taking his men to

*Mexican General
Santa Anna.*

the Alamo as reinforcement. He was caught, however, by the Mexicans on an open prairie close to Coleto Creek.

With odds of three to one against them, the Americans fought until nine were dead and fifty-one were wounded. Then they accepted Urrea's offer of clemency and threw down their guns.

Prisoners were marched back to Fort Goliad and crowded into stockades. Soon new orders came from Santa Anna.

The 342 Americans were formed into a line between two rows of riflemen and systematically shot.

Fannin was the 298th victim of the bloodiest massacre in nineteenth-century American military annals. A few of the wounded men survived to tell the story of the gory day, March 27, 1836.

Although many people east of the Mississippi River soon forgot about Goliad, fighters for the freedom of Texas did not. Time after time, they charged into battle shouting, "Remember Goliad! Remember the Alamo!"

Lawmakers far away in Georgia remembered, too. On January 12, 1854, they named a new county for the martyred hero. Its 396 square miles, today mostly in the Chattahoochee National Forest, are isolated and rugged, just the kind of country that James Walker Fannin liked best.

FANNIN COUNTY

Rugged,
mountainous county
commemorates
James W. Fannin.

6

Spanish Adventurer Offered Christianity for Gold

Shining from the dome of the capitol, Georgia gold catches the eyes of many people passing through Atlanta on interstate highways. Centuries earlier, tales about this yellow metal from the red hills also caught the attention of a self-made Spanish millionaire.

Born poor, Hernando de Soto went to Peru with Pizarro and came home with enough loot to become a favorite of King Charles V and to marry a wealthy woman. However, he still craved riches so he was intrigued by the rumor that somewhere north of Florida, in the region called Guale, gold was so abundant that natives used it to make hats.

In de Soto's grandiose scheme, he would lead followers to the land of gold, where they would become richer than any others who had ever left Europe. He'd relieve the Indians of their uncomfortable metal hats, along with tons of other gold objects.

Instead of robbing the natives, he insisted, he would exchange their yellow metal for the blessings of Christianity. So he enlisted priests and Dominican friars, as well as ambitious young noblemen. Competition to get in on the action was keen. Some men sold everything they had in order to equip themselves. Baltazar de Gallegos parted with houses, vineyards, and ninety ranks of olive trees in order to take part in de Soto's expedition.

Hernando DeSoto.

They left Spain in April of 1538, spending almost one year in Cuba assembling weapons, horses, and pigs. Pigs were self-transporting provisions; they'd go along under their own power until they were needed for food.

Finally the grand expedition landed at what is now Tampa Bay on May 30, 1539. The high point of the debarcation was the moment when the clergy took charge, solemnly placing the paraphernalia of the mass on the soil of the New World. A few months later they held the continent's first Christmas worship service near present-day Tallahassee.

Disappointment was great, however, when no gold was found in Florida and the natives proved hesitant to accept baptism in order to become Christians. Therefore when members of a warlike tribe protested the presence of the Spanish, while crosses gleamed in the sunlight and de Soto bowed in public prayer, fifty captured Indians lost first their noses and then their lives.

By the time de Soto and his followers reached Georgia, crossing the Ocmulgee River near Bainbridge, they had become extremely impatient. Since occasionally they seized from a captured Indian a trinket made of gold, clearly the precious metal was somewhere in the region. Where could the Indians be hiding it?

Somewhere north of Cordele, the gold-seekers were met by an Indian princess and her followers.

"Drawing from over her head a string of pearls," says an ancient account of the meeting, "the beautiful princess put it over the neck of the man whom some Indians were already calling Chief Tyrant. She was the first female ruler that the expedition had met."

The regal bearing of the native woman, plus that string of pearls, gave the Spanish leader an idea. Seizing her, he held her hostage and demanded more pearls plus large quantities of gold.

Gift-bearing Indian princess became a hostage.

Her followers delivered pearls in great quantity, so many that one of the invaders, charged with carrying a huge leather bag full of them, eventually became weary and threw them away. However, it was gold that de Soto really wanted and when it was not forthcoming, the Indian princess was killed somewhere near Augusta in the early summer of 1540.

From there the Spanish meandered back and forth in North Georgia. Frequently the Chief Tyrant climbed into the huge thronelike chair that they carried in order to impress Indians. By now the Europeans had mastered a few words of native dialects, enough to demand at every encounter, "Gold! Gold!"

No one knows precisely what path de Soto followed. There are indications that he passed through Habersham County, where gold was discovered near Duke's Creek centuries later. Whether or not the Spanish attempted to dig in gold-rich country is unknown. If they did so, they dug in the wrong places.

After months of wandering throughout what is now the southeastern United States, the man who had expected to exchange Christianity for gold became the first white man to glimpse the Mississippi River. He crossed it and continued to search futilely for gold, making few converts. When he died in May, 1542, de Soto was buried in secret by his men in the "Father of Waters" so the natives could not desecrate his body. Gold for settlers and Christianity for the Indians came much later in history.

7

Dueling Grounds Saw Blue Blood Flow Like Water

"Our president is a scoundrel and a lying rascal."

Those words, uttered before the Georgia Assembly by General Lachlan McIntosh, were too much for a man of honor to take. Thereupon Council of Safety President Button Gwinnett sent for his friend, George Wells, who agreed to be Gwinnett's second at a duel at dawn and hand delivered a formal note to McIntosh in which Gwinnett demanded "satisfaction accorded a gentleman." He suggested that they meet just before sunrise on the next day, Friday, May 16, 1777.

Although McIntosh grumbled that he wasn't accustomed to rising so early, he agreed to the terms. Honor required that he accept Gwinnett's challenge.

Wells and Major Joseph Habersham, who had consented to serve as McIntosh's second, chose pistols as the weapons that would be used in a meadow near the residence of Royal Governor James Wright.

At the appointed time the antagonists met and "politely saluted one another." As the seconds had not stipulated the distance at which the duelists would stand to fire, Gwinnett indicated that it made no difference to him. McIntosh suggested that eight or ten feet would be sufficient.

Major Habersham, however, insisted upon four full strides, or about twelve feet. Normally, men stood back-to-back as a preface to wheeling and firing, but this time the principals, at the insistence of McIntosh, faced one another with weapons ready to fire at the signal.

Shots rang out almost simultaneously.

Gwinnett dropped to the ground with the cry, "My thigh is broken!" McIntosh, shot through the flesh of his leg, believed his wound to be as serious as that of his opponent and demanded to know if Gwinnett had had enough or was ready for a second shot.

"Yes," indicated Gwinnett, signaling to be raised to take his stand again. Here the seconds stepped between the men and insisted that they exchange perfunctory handshakes.

Button Gwinnett, a signer of the Declaration of Independence and Georgia's chief civil leader, died of his injuries, which led to gangrene.

James Jackson fought twenty-three duels —and lived.

Much of Georgia's bluest blood has been spilled on dueling grounds. During a period of about 120 years after the founding of James Oglethorpe's colony, use of pistols at dawn was the standard way in which a gentleman sought satisfaction for an insult or a wrong.

Just three years after the highly publicized death of Button Gwinnett, a successor in the office he held was challenged by James Jackson. George Wells, who had become interim head of the state government when Richard Howley left the top post in order to attend the Continental Congress, served one of the shortest tenures as Georgia's chief executive, being killed by Jackson in the duel.

Destined to become governor of Georgia and a U.S. Senator, Jackson was the state's most persistent duelist of high rank. He is credited with having fought twenty-three engagements, three of them with a single opponent, attorney Robert Watkins. Tradition says that in one of their encounters Watkins used a dagger as well as a pistol, but he failed to cut down his man.

Another notable duelist was William H. Crawford, a U.S. senator, minister to France, U.S. secretary of war, and U.S. secretary of the treasury. A historical marker on U.S. Highway #78, near Crawfordville, cites his encounters.

Crawford's many duties didn't prevent him from killing P. L. Van Alen in a duel. In another dawn meeting he received a severe wound from Governor John Clark.

Even the president of the United States failed in an attempt to prevent Georgians from fighting. Bad blood between Colonel William Cumming and South Carolina Senator George McDuffie, a native of Georgia, led to taunts and then to a challenge. President James Monroe tried to intervene and make peace between the two prominent men but failed.

Early in the 1820s Cumming and McDuffie met at least four times. Twice they were talked out of firing, but twice they exchanged shots. McDuffie carried Cumming's bullet in his body for the rest of his life.

William H. Crawford killed one opponent.

Finally, to halt the useless waste of life, the legislature enacted a prohibition of dueling, but numerous notables evaded the law by facing their foes in South Carolina. Others simply ignored the statute and met illegally. One of the last such duels was fought near Savannah in August, 1832, when Dr. Philip Minis killed James Jones Stark. The subsequent furor put an end to pistols at dawn.

PART TWO:
Women in Action

8

Cross-Eyed War Queen
of Elbert County

"Go away and leave me alone. I have nothing for King's men; already the villains have stolen all of my pigs. Of poultry, I have nothing left except that old gobbler you see in the yard."

Mrs. Nancy Hart glared at uniformed soldiers who stood at the door of her Elbert County cabin. On a foray from their camp at Augusta, they had crossed Broad River in pursuit of a fugitive. Now they were hungry, as well as tired.

Lifting his musket, a redcoat brought down the barnyard turkey. One of his comrades took it to Nancy and ordered her to clean and cook it without delay.

She grumbled and swore but, with the help of her daughter Sukey, she got the turkey ready for the table. Meanwhile, the Tories whiled away the time teasing ten-year-old Sukey and passing around a jug of fine British whiskey. They bragged about having murdered the "rebellious" Colonel Dooley in bed and made plans for their next expedition.

As soon as the turkey was ready for eating, the soldiers who had crowded into the rough cabin gave full attention to it. Nancy Hart took advantage of the diversion to slip from between some logs a piece of pine used to chink them. One by one, she began passing through the open space the five guns that had been stacked in her cabin.

Two guns were in the clear and Nancy had a third in her

hands when the officer in charge of the Tories detected her stratagem. "Up, men!" he shouted. "We have been betrayed!"

Their hostess whirled around, raising the gun she had planned to drop outside. "Hold still!" she commanded. "I'll kill the first man who moves."

Startled Tories glared at the woman, then exchanged glances among themselves. It was impossible to tell which of the uninvited guests had been chosen as the first target, for Nancy Hart was cross-eyed.

One of the boldest of the redcoats crouched to spring upon the woman. She fired, and he crumpled to the floor. As he slowly died before her eyes, she seized another musket and lifted it into firing position.

"Quick, Sukey," she ordered. "Get that other gun out of the house."

When the child returned from the errand, she informed her mother that "Daddy and the other men are nearly here." She knew perfectly well—but the British did not—that upon hearing that a party of enemy soldiers were in the region, her cowardly father had gone to the nearest canebrake to hide.

Moving into the doorway, Nancy Hart raised her gun. "Surrender your Tory carcasses to a Whig woman, or I'll drop another of you," she commanded.

Still not knowing which one was most likely to be shot next, the redcoats proposed that she accept their surrender "and then shake hands on it." She shook her head, whirling her musket to add to their uncertainty.

The British captives were still standing under her gun when Nancy's husband and the other men of the settlement finally arrived. They suggested shooting the other Tories. She objected. "They surrendered to me," she said, "and shooting is too good for them."

Her suggestion was enough.

Men dragged the dead soldier from the cabin, then took the others into the woods and hanged them one by one.

Sixty years afterward, in 1838, settlers were still showing

visitors the giant oak from which bodies of British soldiers had once dangled. Telling the story of the war queen who had mastered the band, narrators customarily concluded by saying, "Poor cross-eyed Nancy—she was a honey of a patriot, but the devil of a wife!"

Her story reached a national audience through the good offices of a Yankee, Mrs. William H. Ellet, wife of a New York chemistry professor. After her husband joined the faculty of South Carolina College in 1835, she spent fourteen years collecting and polishing orally transmitted lore. *Godey's Lady's Book* for October, 1848, published Mrs. Ellet's account of Nancy Hart's exploit.

Five years later, the fame of the "war woman" was so great that admirers managed to get her surname attached to a newly created county near the northeastern tip of the state. A move to call the county seat Nancyville failed, so a compromise was reached with Hartwell.

Thus in Georgia both a county and a county seat perpetuate the name of "a cross-eyed war queen."

9

Beautiful Widow's Problems Led to the Cotton Gin

"Charleston can wait," teased Caty Greene. "There is much more to see and do here."

Irresolute and less than eager to take up a post of tutor, the only job he could find, Eli Whitney hesitated.

"I'll hear no more of your leaving, for now," his hostess said firmly. She gestured to servants and ordered, "Take Mr. Whitney's things back into the guest bedroom; he will be staying a while."

Whitney, age twenty-seven, did not protest because deep inside, he had hoped to be asked to remain at Mulberry Plantation. Never had he met a woman so provocative as the widow of General Nathanael Greene. Since she had already told Whitney that perhaps he could help her with a vexatious problem whose nature she had not described, he had great hopes for his prospects.

"Life is lonely here," thirty-one-year-old Caty told him as soon as he agreed to remain for a few days. "My husband, Nathanael, died six years ago, and I do so miss the balls and levees we once attended so often."

General Nathanael Greene had put himself in financial straights during his campaign to rid South Carolina of the British. Unable to get funds from the Continental Congress, he had fed and clothed his men out of his own pocket.

When the Revolution was over, Green was nine thousand

pounds in debt. He had failed to receive even partial reimbursement, so when Georgia lawmakers offered to make him a gift of Mulberry Plantation near Savannah as a reward for his military service, he accepted it with gratitude.

When the native of Rhode Island died suddenly at age forty-five, his beautiful twenty-five-year-old widow had to care for the plantation, plus five children. She was deeply in debt.

Visits to creditor Jeremiah Wadsworth of New Jersey led to more loans, but Caty could offer him no payment except herself. Their liaison lasted until Mrs. Wadsworth discovered some of their letters.

High-placed friends did their best to help. Alexander Hamilton, secretary of the treasury, became an intimate advisor, as did secretary of war Henry Knox. George Washington, who had once called her the best dancing partner he'd ever had, tried to intervene on her behalf. In France, the Marquis de Lafayette financed the education of one of her sons.

Nevertheless, in 1792 her troubles were worse than ever. Although Congress had voted to pay her more than $40,000—when the money became available—that wouldn't be enough to meet her pressing debts, as every year the plantation was losing more money. The fine upland cotton it produced was unprofitable because of the laborious work of separating the lint from the seeds.

When the handsome young stranger from New England asked for a night's lodging, Caty persuaded him to stay longer than he had planned; he would break the monotony of plantation life.

Days passed, then weeks. After three months at Mulberry Plantation, Eli Whitney gave up all thought of resuming his journey to Charleston.

Fascinated with Caty, Whitney listened with awe as she talked of long evenings spent dancing with famous men. He laughed with her as she recalled times when she openly flirted with her husband's subordinates. Occasionally Whitney managed to brush against Caty or touch her hand.

Caty Greene gives Eli Whitney a helping hand.

Always, his pulse raced at such encounters. Perhaps if he stayed longer, she might consent to become his wife . . . .

Caty, however, had no intention of marrying him or anyone else because it would be futile to press her claims for money expended by Greene in any role except that of his widow. Neither did she expect to accept Whitney as her lover, as earlier she had turned to Phineas Miller, her overseer. The visitor from Massachussetts would provide a pleasant interlude, no more.

As weeks passed, the young widow Greene discovered that Eli had an inborn mechanical genius. Confronted by a broken farm implement or household object, he spontaneously moved to repair it, seldom spending more than an hour or two doing so.

"If you could devise a machine to pull cotton from seeds, it would make me rich," Whitney's hostess told him one day. Immediately he plunged into the task. This time he did not finish in a few hours, and after a week of intensive effort, he still had gotten nowhere.

Tradition says that as Caty and Eli were strolling one afternoon, she noticed a cat that had been placed in a cage and called Whitney's attention to the animal. Trying to catch a chicken, the animal reached through the slats to grab at the bird. He did not catch it, but pulled back a paw full of feathers into his cage.

Whitney interrupted his walk with his hostess and raced to his workshop, emerging three days later with a model. "Here is the cotton engine you asked me to produce!" he told Caty.

His simple device consisted of two rollers. One was covered with wire spikes like the cat's claws that could reach forward and grab whatever it touched. A second roller, equipped with bristles, rotated close to the first and brushed off the lint.

Abbreviating the name of the engine to cotton "gin," the inventor formed a partnership with Phineas Miller. They built machines and offered to clean, or "gin," cotton for 50 percent of the lint.

However, fortune did not favor them. Blacksmiths and mechanics who saw the cotton gins could quickly duplicate them. And although Whitney had applied for a patent, he didn't receive one until numerous imitations of his gin were in use. Later he was rewarded with $50,000 by South Carolina, but he spent it—and more—trying to defend his patent rights.

Caty Greene finally received a partial financial settlement from Congress. She invested some of it in Whitney's gin, only to see the money disappear.

Desperate, the still dazzling widow Greene bought heavily when shares of Yazoo, Mississippi, land companies were offered for sale. Georgia legislators, who sold about thirty-five million acres of Yazoo land to speculators for $500,000, did not have clear title to the land, so revocation of the Yazoo sale left Caty Greene "feeling like a plucked chicken." At least $60,000 in debt, she gave up her plantation and took refuge on Cumberland Island. Her death there at age sixty ended a true-life drama in which development of the cotton gin was but one episode.

10

Sophy Hopkey Was Crucial to the Start of the Methodist Movement

Like nearly everyone else in Savannah, Sophy Hopkey was eager to get a look at the colony's newly-arrived missionary. She was one of twenty persons on hand when the Reverend John Wesley, M.A., first administered Holy Communion in Georgia. Neither she nor Wesley ever forgot the date: Saturday, March 13, 1736.

Sophy was one of the few eligible females in James Oglethorpe's infant colony. At eighteen she wasn't bothered by the clergyman's short stature or his face, already stern at age 33. To her, he symbolized all that was romantic about faraway England.

Within weeks, Sophy put timidity aside and sought advice from General Oglethorpe. Responding to her questions, the founder of Georgia said he thought Mr. Wesley would like her best in white, the color symbolizing purity.

That's why Sophy wore white when she attended early morning prayers at Wesley's house, then remained to have breakfast with him and a colleague. Soon she was also present at evening prayers, radiant in pure white. When she expressed a desire to learn French, linguist Wesley graciously offered to spend an hour a day teaching her.

Although Wesley had come to Georgia to convert Indians to Christianity, that mission proved unsuccessful and it seemed fitting that he inconvenience himself a bit for a girl

The Rev. John
Wesley, M. A.

whom he described as "often the most affected of listeners."
Furthermore, her aunt was married to the colony's magistrate.

Rising daily at 4:00 A.M. for an hour of prayer and Scripture reading, Wesley frequently stopped during the day for five or ten minutes of renewed prayer. Wednesdays and Fridays were days of fasting and penance.

Soon the clergyman's fast-expanding diary began to include more and longer references to Miss Sophy. He confessed to himself that he was frightened at realizing that not all of his thoughts were directed to the salvation of his own soul and to the spiritual welfare of his flock. To make matters worse, he believed that Miss Sophy was showing signs of being interested in him as a male, not simply as a pastor.

As their relationship grew more intimate, Wesley's notations in his diary grew more tortured. Then they spent six days and nights together, traveling by boat the one hundred miles from Frederica to Savannah. In bad weather they slept crowded together with the crew of four and the lone other passenger. Wesley entertained Sophy by reading to her from Patrick's *Prayers* and Fleury's *History of the Church.*

Back in Savannah, his diary for December 19, 1736, included impassioned entries. He exhorted himself "in the name of God, to be more watchful, before and in prayer; Not to touch even her clothes by choice; think not of her."

However, he could not get Sophy out of his mind, even during hours of fasting and penance. Nor could he fail to be aware that Masters Tom Mellichamp and William Williamson had shown clear, and not totally innocent, interest in her. Naively he thought perhaps he should warn her.

Had they not been so fateful, events of 1737 would seem like scenes from a comic opera.

Wesley was repeatedly on the brink of proposing the marriage that he was sure Sophy eagerly desired. Always, though, he stopped short of taking the fateful step from which there would be no turning back. Wesley could not drive Sophy from his mind, but he could not bring himself to ask for her hand.

Then Sophy Hopkey married William Williamson on Saturday, March 12, 1737, exactly one year from the day she and John Wesley first saw one another.

Mrs. Williamson remained a member of Wesley's parish, and he began to warn and then admonish her to be more zealous in her religious duties, "owning her fault and declaring her repentance." She ignored his exhortations. A month after her marriage, Wesley refused to admit her to a service of Holy communion.

On the following day—August 8, 1737—Pastor Wesley was served with a warrant charging him with "defaming said Sophy" and asking damages in the sum of one thousand pounds. Magistrate Thomas Causton preferred additional charges. Forty-four males who made up a grand jury pondered the evidence, then voted a lengthy true bill against the pastor.

Wesley fled from Savannah to Charleston on foot.

Wesley asked for a formal trial but did not get it. A new court order commanded him to remain in Savannah and to post surety of fifty pounds. Not having that sum, the man who had come as a missionary fled in the night, describing himself as "a prisoner at large."

Back in England, the exile from Georgia felt himself to be a total failure. Guilt and despair drove him to a prayer meeting in Aldersgate Street, London. There a profound religious experience turned him into an evangelist.

Had Sophy Hopkey been more patient or more persuasive, she might have become the bride of an obscure Anglican priest. Instead it can be argued that she was one of the important factors in John Wesley's launching the world-wide Methodist movement.

11

Slave Girl Triggered First Big North/South Split

"I don't want to go to that country in a ship," Kitty insisted. "I don't know nobody there. This is my home."

With George W. Lane accompanying him as a witness, Emory College President A. B. Longstreet had made a carefully worded offer. If the young slave belonging to Bishop James O. Andrew of Oxford would only say the word, she could go free.

Conditions were attached, of course. She could not stay in Georgia, state law would not permit that. She could go North to a "free state," where she would find herself alone and helpless. Or she could rejoin her compatriots in Africa.

Common sense seemed to dictate that if she chose freedom she should make "a long trip by water" to Liberia.

Frightened at the prospect of leaving behind everyone she knew and loved, Kitty shook her head firmly as the offer was repeated three times. "No," she said, "I sure don't want to go across the ocean and be free."

Like other slaves she had no surname, but everyone in Newton County knew that an old lady of Augusta had willed her to Bishop Andrew who had become one of five bishops of the Methodist Episcopal Church in 1832.

Kitty was left to him because her owner was confident that he would care for her like a member of the family. What's more, he had solemnly promised to offer her freedom when she became nineteen.

That decisive point in her life was reached in 1842, but by then Georgia lawmakers had enacted new statutes forbidding the practice of permitting freed slaves to remain in the state. Until then the number of free blacks had grown by the natural children of plantation owners gaining their freedom at the death of their masters who were also their fathers, or by freed men moving from other states, or by slaves purchasing their own freedom. Growing fear of insurrection led political leaders to mandate that manumission, or freedom, meant exile.

Keenly aware of the alternatives, Kitty never wavered during discussions about her future. Oxford was home, and she preferred to remain in the Andrew household as a slave.

Neither she nor other villagers had the slightest idea that her decision would trigger the first major North/South split, sixteen years before the outbreak of civil war.

Methodists who converged upon New York's Greene Street Church on May 1, 1844, to discuss slavery knew that sectional differences would be hotly debated. Although only members of the clergy came as voting delegates, they represented 985,598 whites, 145,409 blacks, and 4,129 American Indians, making their church the largest religious body in the United States. Decisions made by Methodists would have implications for the whole nation.

Parliamentary jockeying lasted for several days. Southern delegates, sensing that a showdown was at hand, wished to avoid it, while anti-slavery forces were confident that they had a slight, but decisive, advantage.

As the Methodists debated, delegates to the Anti-Slavery Society's annual meeting convened a few blocks away. In the chair was William Lloyd Garrison, whose name was hated in the South. His fiery *Emancipator* newspaper, launched in 1831, had evoked an unparalleled reaction, even causing Georgia lawmakers to offer a reward of $1,000 for his capture.

With the fiery abolitionist presiding, his followers took

action aimed at persuading undecided Methodists. By a three-to-one vote, the society urged "immediate dissolution of the existing union between Northern Freedom (such as it is) and Southern Slavery."

Methodists established a special committee "to investigate a report that one of our bishops has become connected with slavery." While delegates debated, Andrew tried to resign, but his colleagues wouldn't let him do so.

However, a formal report finding him guilty of slaveholding and recommending his suspension from office evoked a minority protest from thirteen states. Soon the protest coalesced into a Plan of Separation.

Formal North/South division came within a year.

At its organization on May 1, 1845, the Methodist Episcopal Church, South, claimed 332,067 white members along with 124,961 blacks and 2,972 Indians. A precedent and a pattern had been established. Soon the nation would see a similar division that would mean war.

After refusing to go to Liberia, Kitty was given a simple cottage in which she lived with her husband, Nathan. It was moved to Salem Campground, near Covington, in 1938, where it stands today as a mute witness to forces larger than the persons who set them in motion.

Fiery abolitionists from New England made no effort to find for Kitty a home where she could be free with dignity. Bishop Andrew and his supporters did not attempt to provide funds that would enable her to go somewhere other than Africa.

Forced by law to choose among the North, far away Liberia, and a comfortably familiar life with her master and his family, a girl of nineteen chose slavery, setting the stage for the War That Should Not Have Been.

12

Savannah Socialite Launched the Girl Scouts of America

"Juliette, there's no other hostess in London like you," said a frequent guest. "Every time we dine together, I eat Georgia ham and yams."

Mrs. Willy Low, widow of a multimillionaire, took her friend's statement as a compliment. "You're right," she admitted. "What's more, this is the only place you can listen to a mockingbird sing while you eat an ice made from Ogeechee limes!"

Besides the food and the music of a bird, her household was distinctive as being the center for a group of people who studied sculpture zealously at night. One of the devotees was a new male friend of the hostess, Robert Stephenson Smyth Baden-Powell.

Descended from a distinguished family, Baden-Powell had served with distinction in Parliament before going to Africa in uniform. During the Boer War he was in command at Mafeking, 160 miles west of Pretoria. Encircled and besieged, the town held out for an incredible 217 days, and a grateful government made him a major general and created him Baron of Gilwell.

Convinced by his army experiences that boys needed more physical and outdoor training, he launched a movement that became the Boy Scouts. Then with his sister Agnes, he formed an equal-but-separate organization of Girl

Juliette Gordon Low in uniform.

Guides. By-laws of the two groups forbade Girl Guides and Boy Scouts to speak to each other while in uniform.

However, nothing barred long and intimate conversations between would-be sculptors Baden-Powell and Mrs. Low.

When her lengthy stay in England came to an end, Juliette Low crossed the Atlantic on the same steamer with Lord Baden-Powell. However, on the voyage he became interested in a younger woman (whom he later married), and Juliette left the ship in Jamaica, their first landfall.

She already had made up her mind to bring the Girl Guides to America and on the day she reached Savannah, she contacted a cousin, Nina Pape. "I've got something for the girls of Savannah and all America and all the world. And we're going to start it tonight!" she exclaimed.

Searching for a starting point, the two women thought of a distant relative, youthful Page Anderson who was already leader of a group of nature enthusiasts. She was cajoled, or strong-armed, into agreeing to serve as captain of a patrol. Then Juliette Low solemnly initiated fifteen other young girls into the Girl Guides, which met in the carriage house behind her home. Uniforms she prescribed consisted of dark blue skirts, middy blouses, black cotton stockings, and black hair ribbons.

Growing rapidly, the movement launched in Savannah soon had a change in name. It became Girl Scouts of America when a national headquarters was set up in Washington, D.C., in 1915.

Eleanor Nash, sister of poet Ogden Nash, said of her, "Juliette Low has a wicked wit and a charm that I am too word poor to describe. She is quicksilver and pepper—leavened with humanity and laughter. She is the person I most like to be with."

Today, Juliette Low's birthplace in Savannah is a shrine for the three million girls and their adult leaders who form Girl Scouts of America, and in the state capitol in Atlanta is a bust of "The Woman from Savannah"—a tad less severe looking than when photographed in uniform.

Although Juliette Low was never allied with the movement for women's rights, it was she who liberated millions of girls by giving them their first taste of camping, backpacking, and other activities long regarded as exclusively for males. No wonder she is the sole woman in the Georgia Hall of Fame in the state capitol!

13

Emily Harrison Saved a Forest for a City

"Let that tulip poplar lie where it fell," directed Emily Harrison. "Change the footpath to go around the tree."

Diminutive in size and deceptively mild in appearance, the DeKalb County woman betrayed her steel-hard determination only by a slight rasp in her voice. She didn't fight with a gun or a knife. She used words. Her fiercest opponents were not British redcoats or blue-clad Union soldiers. They were developers.

Through the influence of the woman whom long-time friends called Miss Emily, Fernbank Forest has no close rival. It is a large tract of virgin woodland in the heart of metropolitan Atlanta, which is expanding so rapidly that "development" seems to be nearly out of control.

The story could have been quite different.

"Everyone acquainted with the forest and its story knows it was not easy to save," said Decatur attorney James A. Mackay. "Developers were falling all over one another in their eagerness to buy the tract. It was the last really large parcel of untouched land in the central metro area.

"Real estate brokers and housing complex developers failed only because a strong-minded woman led a handful of people who wanted to save the trees, flowers, and birds."

Courthouse records concerning the land that includes the forest go back to 1824, when the county was just two years

old. Zador D. Harrison became owner in 1881 and on it built
a cottage, the first residence on the property.

Harrison's daughter, Emily, was seven when they moved
into a house so small it did not significantly affect the forest.
At age ten she persuaded her father to put up a twenty-room
manor.

When Zador Harrison died in 1935, he left an estate that
was to be divided among ten heirs. One of them—Emily—
moved into action at once because she feared that the forest
would be cut down in order to create a subdivision. Such a
turn of events would, in her words, "forever ruin this place
as an outdoor schoolroom for children of future generations."

Miss Emily recruited Dr. W. D. Baker, Emory University
biologist, and persuaded him to write newspaper articles, as
well as talk to civic clubs at every opportunity. With their
followers they formed Fernbank, Inc., and managed to purchase the entire Harrison tract for $35,000.

Since in order to turn the forest into an outdoor schoolroom, the nonprofit corporation needed money, a New York
natural history agency was retained to help develop plans
and to secure funds. One representative wanted to use the
property to raise dogs. Another proposed that much or all of
the forest be developed as a zoo. Someone else wanted to
grow persimmons on a commercial scale. But little or no
money came to the trustees.

For years the Fernbank trustees didn't know quite what to
do with the forest that had been saved. Then Jim Cherry,
county superintendent of schools, came forward with a pro-
posal. As a result, in 1964 a forty-eight-year lease was
signed. Under its terms, the virgin forest was to become a
living laboratory as part of the county school system.

Miss Emily continued to live in the forest until 1941,
when at age sixty-seven, she moved into an apartment. She
continued regularly to spend much of her time there until
her death at age ninety-nine.

Still truly virginal, Fernbank Forest is the only one of its kind in the Piedmont Plateau that stretches from Alabama to New York. Even in the famous Smoky Mountains National Park, there has been extensive logging during this century.

Not so, Fernbank. Many of its fine trees were sturdy when James Oglethorpe brought the first English settlers to Georgia in 1732. Poplar, oaks, hickories, and pines predominate.

Native ferns abound. Other varieties, like the Christmas fern, were transplanted by Miss Emily.

On a tract adjoining the forest that Miss Emily saved there is now a science center, complete with an astronomical observatory and planetarium. A natural history museum, whose construction began a half-century after Miss Emily's death, makes the Fernbank complex unlike any other in the nation operated by a public school system.

If Miss Emily could only know, her sparkling eyes—blue as the periwinkles that carpet forest slopes in March—would reveal her triumph at having beaten "the big money men who'd have cut down 300-year-old trees for the sake of one more shopping mall."

PART THREE:
The Joy of Battle

Emma Sansom rode behind General Forrest.

14

Emma Sansom Pointed Out the Trail

"I told him I knew of a trail where our cows used to cross in low water," Emma Sansom recalled. Continuing her recollection of her dramatic encounter with Confederate General Nathan Bedford Forrest, she said, "I told him I believed he could get his men across there, and that if he'd put my saddle on a horse, I would show him the way."

Cavalry leader Forrest responded, "There's no time to saddle a horse; get up here, behind me!"

He rode close to the bank on which the girl was standing, and she jumped on the animal behind him. When Emma's mother took alarm, Forrest promised to bring her back safely as he prodded his horse into a gallop.

That hasty encounter took place close to the end of what many call the most unusual raid of the Civil War.

Leading a band of two thousand Union fighting men—mounted, not on horses but on mules—Colonel A. D. Streight hoped to cut vital Confederate rail lines in North Georgia. However, his ambitious 1863 raid ran into trouble when General Nathan B. Forrest, leading a much smaller force, began dogging his heels.

Although Forrest couldn't hope to win in an all-out battle, he could keep his enemy moving so the Federals would become too exhausted to fight.

Indeed, by May 2, more than anything else the Union Soldiers needed rest. Nevertheless, after crossing Alabama's Black Warrior River, men in blue turned toward the Coosa River and Rome, Georgia, an important rail center and a major objective of their foray.

After a minor skirmish at Big Will's Creek, the Yankees reached Black Creek. Originating on Lookout Mountain, the stream is small, but crooked, cold, and provided by nature with steep clay banks and a soft mud bottom. In 1863, a single uncovered wooden bridge was the only means of crossing it without a detour of many miles through extremely rough country.

After crossing the rickety bridge, Streight burned it, led his men a safe distance into a dense cover of trees, and told them, at last, they could get a little rest. His thinking was that the Confederates would be stymied on the far side of Black Creek, in Alabama. It would take them several hours to make a crossing, and then they would be the exhausted ones when they came in sight of Union forces.

Just as Streight expected, Forrest dashed up to the stream and surveyed the burned bridge with dismay. That was when he met the farm girl.

Born in Georgia's Walton County in 1847, Emma Sansom had lived on Black Creek just one year, but she had learned the country well. Riding behind Forrest, she guided him to the ford where her cows sometimes crossed. As she dismounted, the rebel leader asked for her name and a lock of her hair.

Forrest then led his weary cavalrymen across Black Creek. Within minutes, rather than hours, they made contact with the mule-riding Union forces.

Across the fateful creek, Streight had come upon the roughest terrain he had yet encountered. A munitions plant in Rome required huge quantities of charcoal. To produce it, workmen had felled trees in an area that covered several square miles. Stumps and litter made movement slow, and crisscrossing wagon roads prevented the finding of a proper trail.

Emma Sansom.

Streight and his weary men crossed the Chattooga River and worked their way toward Rome. Calculating that by burning the Black Creek bridge he had gained a good half day, he felt that a few hours of rest would put his men in shape to attack the city of Rome. Meanwhile, his scouts surveyed Rome from a distance and reported it heavily fortified.

While Streight debated his next move, Forrest and his riders surrounded the Yankee camp, closing in during the early hours of May 3. Many Union soldiers were so weary that they continued to sleep even after volleys had been fired. After a brief parley, the Federals surrendered, though they outnumbered their pursuers by four to one.

Nathan Bedford Forrest seldom bothered to write anything, not even battle orders, but this occasion was special. He tore a stained page from a memorandum book and on it wrote a note of thanks to Emma Sansom. Then he rode off on his fine horse, carrying the lock of her hair with him.

Eighteen months later, Emma married Confederate soldier C. B. Johnson and went with him to live in Texas at war's end.

In 1899 the Alabama legislature gave Emma a square mile of land "as a token of admiration and gratitude" for her foresight and heroism. Even more than the land, she treasured the memory of the day when she rode toward battle lines behind one of America's finest cavalry commanders.

15

Leonidas Polk Dispensed Holy Water on Bloody Ground

"We've waited long enough. I am ready, as soon as I have conferred with General Johnston," said General John B. Hood.

Leonidas Polk of Louisiana, simultaneously a Confederate general and an Episcopal bishop, nodded understanding and agreement. "I will wait as long as necessary," he promised.

Hood left his own quarters in Dalton, Georgia, and went to the headquarters of his commander, Joseph E. Johnston, where he remained until after midnight.

General Polk, wearing a stained surplice over an old gray hunting shirt, had removed his usual slouched hat and sabre for the occasion. While waiting, he observed that Hood's room was simply furnished. It had only a mess table and four rickety chairs. A single candle provided light.

Polk had found a battered tin basin, into which he had poured a cup of water. Hood entered the room awkwardly, his leg having been amputated close to his hip. A splendid cork leg bought for him in Europe was of little help in walking.

"You may sit, if you like," said Bishop-General Polk.

"No, I prefer to stand, if that is agreeable," said the crippled soldier. Leaning on his crutches, John B. Hood bowed his head reverently as the Bishop of Louisiana made the sign of the cross over him.

That middle-of-the-night baptismal service, performed in the heat of Confederate retreat toward Atlanta under the onslaught of greatly superior Union forces, was America's first battlefield baptism of a general by a general.

The second act of the drama followed quickly.

Knowing nothing of Hood's baptism, Mrs. Joseph E. Johnston, wife of Hood's commander with whom he frequently and violently differed, wrote from Atlanta to General Polk:

> You are never too much occupied, I well know, to pause to perform a good deed. General Johnston has never been baptized. It is the dearest wish of my heart that he should be, and that you should perform the ceremony would be a great gratification to me. I am writing to him on the subject, and am sure he waits only your leisure. I rejoice that you are near him in these trying times. May God crown all your efforts with success, and spare your life for your country and friends.

On the night he received Mrs. Johnston's letter, Polk went to his commander's tent. There he was surprised, but gratified, to learn that Hood also wanted to be present for the

John B. Hood, first general to receive battlefield baptism at the hands of another general.

ceremony. Everyone in the Confederate army knew that Hood was jealous of Johnston and had sent highly critical reports about him to Richmond.

A tolerant and kindly man, Johnston was pleased that Hood wished to attend. General William J. Hardee was also present as Johnston's official sponsor.

When they all had gathered at the commander's headquarters, Johnston knelt and received the rite of Holy Baptism. It was Georgia's—and the nation's—second battlefield baptism of a general by a general. This time, each of the four persons present for the ceremony wore Confederate uniforms and insignia of rank.

Less than a month later, three of the four rode up Pine Mountain to survey the terrain. Hood did not accompany them, as he was busy reading scouting reports of nearby enemy movements.

General William T. Sherman had paused momentarily, on top of a smaller hill about a quarter of a mile from Pine Mountain. Peering through field glasses, he was irritated to discover that the high ground was already occupied by men in gray.

Sherman turned to a colonel of artillery and ordered: "Have one of your best gunners throw a shell over there and break up that congregation!" At his command, a subordinate aimed a 12-pound Parrott gun. Then a sergeant yanked the lanyard.

Before the roar of the big gun reached Pine Mountain, the three Confederate generals reined their horses to descend the slope. As they moved forward, a cannon ball hit Bishop-General Leonidas Polk in the chest.

The clergyman, who twice baptized his fellow generals within earshot of Yankee artillery, was the only one of the trio to die on the battlefield. Both Hood and Johnston fought for the duration of the Civil War, reassured by knowledge that if they should fall, they would die as baptized believers.

16

Oglethorpe's "Indian Ways" Stopped Spain Cold

"As Georgia goes, so will all of British North America. May God be with us in these crucial times."

These sentiments echoed over and over in letters of James Oglethorpe, about 250 years ago. Georgia, youngest and weakest of Britain's North American colonies, was just nine years old. There was no certainty that she would endure.

Early in his stay in Georgia, Oglethorpe decided that the Spanish—not the French, as most Europeans said—threatened the future of the colony. Therefore at every opportunity he detailed an early version of a "domino theory." If Georgia should fall to the Spanish, he argued, invaders would move up the coast. South Carolina would be seized, then North Carolina. Before the Spanish tide ceased to flow, the flag of King Philip would fly all the way from Saint Augustine to Cape Cod.

Seeming to prove Oglethorpe correct, a fleet of Spanish ships carrying veteran soldiers left Cuba on May 26, 1742. After a halt at Saint Augustine, the invaders reached Georgia waters on July 1. James Oglethorpe, a veteran of European wars, withdrew from most outposts. Saint Simons Island, he decided, was the place to make a stand.

Florida's Governor Montiano, commanding the vastly superior attacking force, signalled for his fleet to launch an assault about 7:00 A.M. on July 5. They entered Saint Simons sound without resistance and effected an orderly landing.

Then Montiano, who was in no hurry, waited until July 7 to begin moving toward the island's only strong position, Fort Frederica. He expected the forthcoming battle to proceed according to the established European system of combat with troops deployed in well-ordered ranks.

However, Georgia's founder had spent much time with his Indian friends and allies, learning from them the basic concepts of guerilla warfare. Hence, he ignored continental military manuals.

About five miles from Frederica, the attackers would have to cross a marsh on a narrow trail, so there, not at the little fort, Oglethorpe chose to make a stand. He stationed his ragged sharpshooters in dense woods that bordered the marsh.

Oglethorpe's sharpshooters fired from ambush.

The Spanish troops knew Frederica to be small and weak, easily mastered they thought. Headed toward the fort, they moved forward in orderly ranks until they reached the marsh and had to form a thin column to negotiate the trail.

There the members of the tiny Georgia militia, their Indian allies, and a handful of British regulars fired from ambush. A few invaders fell, the rest panicked and fled.

Though no English blood and little Spanish was spilled that day, the engagement became noted as the Battle of Bloody Marsh.

In its aftermath, one of Oglethorpe's French-born soldiers deserted to the enemy. Georgia's founder—a perennial gambler—decided upon a risky ploy. He forged a note addressed to the deserter. Supposedly confidential, it indicated that a vast English fleet would reach Georgia within hours.

Oglethorpe gave the bogus message to a Spanish prisoner, whom he released upon his oath that he'd deliver it to the Frenchman and no one else. Montiano's aides, reasoned Oglethorpe, would be sure to search the man.

They did.

Fearful of attack by British warships that didn't exist, the Spanish kept a sharp lookout to sea. When masts were glimpsed at a distance, their worst fears seemed to be confirmed. In a state of near-panic, the Spanish commander evacuated Saint Simons Island and ordered his ships and men to return to home bases in Florida and Cuba.

No list of great battles of the Western world includes Bloody Marsh. Yet the skirmish and its aftermath proved to be decisive. Spain never again attempted a military invasion of North America.

17

Future Emperor Learned Art of War at Savannah

"You, boy, fall out!"

Splendid in his elaborate uniform, Count Charles Hector D'Estaing gestured as he spoke.

"No," replied a would-be member of D'Estaing's Volunteer Chasseurs. Instead of obeying the signal given by the French commander, he drew himself to his full six feet, four inches. "I am young," said the barefoot black. "But I am no boy. I can fight with the best."

He paused, eyed the European, and added, "Besides, no one hates the British as much as I do."

It was his closing comment that won him a place in the force being recruited. As admiral of French forces, D'Estaing had fought the British on several seas during the great European conflict of the mid-eighteenth century known as the Seven Years War. Then when France became an ally of the rebellious American colonies, D'Estaing was given command of a New World fleet in 1778, with the real purpose of trying to thwart Britain again. His immediate goal was to take the vital port of Savannah.

To do this D'Estaing assembled a fleet of thirty-six ships at a base in the West Indies, accepting black recruits such as the fourteen-year-old who had announced his hatred for the British.

Actually Christophe, which was his only name, did not

Future sovereign, Christophe.

hate the British more than he did the French, or any other white people. The western third of his Caribbean island home of Saint Dominque (Hispaniola) had been ceded by Spain to France in 1697 and the French colonists had made it a prosperous holding by importing many African slaves for their big coffee and spice plantations.

Harsh taskmasters, the French earned the enmity of their black underlings, so the brilliant and cunning Christophe was taking this opportunity to learn the art of war, white man's style.

"I saw my first game of French skittles when I was eleven," he said in later years. "Planters amused themselves with it. They would bury a Negro in sand up to his neck, then roll cannonballs at his face."

At Savannah, Christophe got all he was looking for, and more. British commander Augustine Prevost had only 2,500 men, but all were sheltered by sturdy fortifications. They were more than ready when attacking forces launched an

Siege of Savannah as depicted by a contemporary artist.

all-out effort on October 9, 1779. During one day of hand-to-hand fighting, French and American losses topped 1,000 men. Their casualties included Count Casimir Pulaski, the Polish hero, who died of his wounds and Pierre L'Enfant, who recovered and later designed the city of Washington, D.C. Christophe was also wounded.

Although on the losing side at Savannah, the young black man learned much about strategy and the use of weapons. Never able to read or write, he could not make notes, but he was a keen observer with a sharp memory.

Twelve years later, during the French Revolution, the slaves of Saint Dominque launched their own rebellion, eventually proclaiming their colony the independent country of Haiti in 1804. The man who had been a raw recruit at Savannah was a leading general in the fight for Haitian independence. He had learned his lessons in the art of warfare well. His soldiers—plus yellow fever—proved too much even for Napoleon's veterans.

Christophe seized control of the new nation and assumed the title of Henry I, King of the North, ruling with an iron hand until 1820—the only crowned king to take part in Georgia's fight for independence.

18

Nashville's Father Bliemel Died at Jonesboro

"We need you, Father. Lots more than the women and children do. It won't be long before we're facing Yankee guns. Please face them with us . . ."

That line of reasoning, varying slightly in language but constant in meaning, was expressed over and over. It came from the men of the heavily German parish of the Assumption in Nashville, Tennessee.

Pastor Emmeran Bliemel, a Benedictine priest, was deeply stirred and could not question the logic of the fighting men. Undoubtedly some in the parish he served would be wounded, and others would die in battle.

Nashville and its environs had already been the scene of skirmishes when occupied by Federal troops in the spring of 1862. Split down the middle in terms of citizens' loyalty, Tennessee was filled with pro-Union groups in spite of having adopted an ordinance of secession.

Although Bavarian-born Bliemel, age thirty-one, had only a hazy understanding of the issues leading to the Civil War, he clearly understood that he had taken a vow to devote his life to God and his fellow men. Fidelity to that vow never wavered. Therefore, it was inevitable that he follow his men into battle to bring spiritual solace to the living and final rites to the dying.

At Clinton, Mississippi, in October, 1862, the Nashville

men elected Emmeran Bliemel to serve them as their chaplain. This was an entirely unofficial action, as Father Bliemel's request for leave had been rejected by his bishop, and no commission had been issued him by the Confederate War Department.

However, when news reached Nashville of the battles of Chickamauga and Lookout Mountain, Bliemel again requested permission to join his men in uniform, and this time his superiors yielded.

Since railroad travel to the south had been suspended, except for military forces, the only way to get from Nashville to Dalton, Georgia, where the Tenth Tennessee had gone into winter quarters, was by horse.

Taking a roundabout route, and doing much of his riding

Rebels captured at Jonesboro were marched to Atlanta.

at night on an animal donated by the Catholics of McEwen, Tennessee, Father Bliemel reached Dalton in November and received a heart-warming reception as unofficial chaplain.

Augustin Verot, Catholic Bishop of Georgia, sent a memorandum giving his approval to the priest's service in the military camp. Ninety days later, he won official appointment as a chaplain in the Army of the Confederate States of America.

After Atlanta fell, the Tenth Tennessee moved twenty miles south, to Jonesboro. Outnumbered perhaps six to one by fast-approaching Yankees, they hoped to hold the vital Macon and Western Railroad, with hastily prepared fortifications along the rail line giving them a defensive advantage.

August 31, 1864, saw the first day of fighting in the Battle of Jonesboro as Sherman's determined men cut Atlanta's last supply line. Many Tennesseans died, and more were wounded. One who was mortally wounded was the regiment's commander, Colonel William Grace.

Chaplain Bliemel rushed to the side of the dying officer to administer last rites. While praying with and for Grace, eyewitnesses later reported, "his head was blown off by enemy fire."

A battlefield casualty at age thirty-two, the Bavarian who died at Jonesboro was the first Catholic priest in America's history to die in combat.

19

For Once, Sherman Was a Gentleman

"Tonight we are camped near Cassville," wrote a battle-weary Union soldier on May 18, 1864. "Our forces . . . [will] meet the enemy somewhere near the town."

Neither statement, it turned out, was correct and he was not to know or understand a poignant event that did take place there, one very much out of keeping with the public reputation of his commander, General William Tecumseh Sherman.

In the first place, the Georgia town was not Cassville, although the local citizens had failed to so inform the Union army. Earlier the county seat and Cass County had been named in honor of Lewis Cass, secretary of war in Andrew Jackson's administration. However, when it later was revealed that Cass had been reluctant to fight in the War of 1812, public sentiment preferred a name change. Thus when Savannah-born Francis Bartow became the first high-ranking casualty of the Civil War, that provided the necessary impetus to change names. Cass County became Bartow County, and the town of Cassville became Manassas to commemorate the battle where Bartow died (it was called Bull Run by the Yankees).

In the second place, enemy forces did not meet at Manassas, Georgia, as the Union letter writer predicted. Confederate General Joseph E. Johnston and his army slipped away during the hours of darkness on May 20.

However, General Sherman's scorched earth policy prevailed, just as it did elsewhere on the wide swath of the march from Atlanta to the sea. Torching the towns truly made war a hell, as the general later recalled.

Yet one home was spared.

B. A. Botkin, in his *Civil War Treasury*, quotes the note tacked to the door of the house that was not burned:

> Dear Madam,
>
> You once said that you would pity the man who would ever become my enemy. My answer was that I would ever protect and shield you. That I have done. Forgive me all else. I am but a soldier.
>
> Respectfully,
W. T. Sherman

What did the note mean?

Twenty years earlier, in the spring of 1844, Sherman, who

General William T. Sherman (seated with arms crossed) and his generals. Jefferson C. Davis, commander of the XIVth corps, stands at Sherman's right.

Cecilia Stovall.

was then a junior officer, had spent several weeks in Georgia helping to settle claims that grew out of the Seminole Wars. There he had renewed acquaintance with Augusta-born Cecilia Stovall. They had first met when the Southern belle had visited her brother, a classmate of Sherman's at West Point.

The story is that "Cump," as Cecilia called the young army officer, was very much in love, but his suit was rejected. Yet he continued to love her through the years.

That is why, tradition says, the one home in Manassas, Georgia, was spared destruction, for it belonged to Mrs. Shellman, the former Cecilia Stovall.

PART FOUR:
Innocence and Guilt

Last American slave ship, Savannah-based Wanderer.

20

Last Slaver Boasted He Couldn't Be Convicted

"If Franklin Pierce and his whole cabinet were here," Charles Augustus Lafayette Lamar of Savannah wrote to a fellow conspirator, "they could not convict me. A man of influence can do as he pleases."

Relatives and friends warned that he might wind up in the penitentiary or in a lunatic asylum. Either way, the famous Lamar name would be blackened.

However, Charles Augustus made it clear that he intended to test laws he considered unconstitutional. Under statutes enacted in 1807 and later, a person who engaged in the African slave trade was subject to trial on charges of piracy.

"Piracy, indeed!" he snorted. Edicts such as that constituted "gross infringements upon the rights of free individuals." Partly to provide a test case, the wealthy Savannah business leader let it be known that he planned to send a ship to Africa for a cargo of blacks.

Upon reflection, Lamar decided that one ship was not enough. He might as well make a good profit from the venture; therefore, he'd send three vessels.

Georgia-born Howell Cobb, serving as U.S. secretary of the treasury, was married to a cousin of Lamar. When he got wind of the plans, Cobb sent a stern warning. Piracy fell under his personal jurisdiction, he said. Though he strongly sympathized with the cause of slave owners, he intended to enforce the letter of the law. Conviction of piracy carried a mandatory death sentence, he pointed out.

Lamar ignored warnings from Cobb and others and outfitted three vessels, as planned. If either the *E. A. Rawlins* or the *Richard Cobden* reached Africa and returned with a full cargo, which is uncertain, slaves were landed in Cuba.

No so with the third vessel.

In New York early in the summer of 1858, Lamar's agent had bought a splendid 234-ton schooner, whose slim lines and high masts made her one of the fastest ships afloat. On November 28, 1858, the *Wanderer* docked at Jekyll Island after her round-trip to the Dark Continent. From her cargo of nearly 500 slaves, 409 had survived the crossing. Lamar moved so swiftly that slaves were widely dispersed to plantations before federal agents knew they had been landed.

Noted Savannah attorney Henry R. Jackson was selected to serve as special prosecutor when Lamar was put on trial. Howell Cobb, bidding to become the Democratic nominee for the presidency, put his official and personal influence behind the prosecution.

Formal legal action began in November, 1859. By then, it was clear that overwhelming popular support was on the side of the defendants, Lamar and colleagues.

A federal marshal identified and seized a band of blacks who had been brought on the *Wanderer*. However, Lamar not only managed to retrieve his property, he had the lawmen who drove the wagons loaded with contraband humans arrested. Then these agents were charged by Lamar with having stolen domestic slaves.

Sixteen distinguished Savannah citizens who made up the jury could not stomach a verdict under whose terms Lamar might hang. They cleared him of piracy, but convicted him on minor charges. America's last slaver was fined five hundred dollars and sentenced to thirty days' confinement. He spent his jail term in his own comfortable quarters.

By then, it was clear that South Carolina might do much more than simply talk about secession, so Lamar began forming a company of volunteers to go to the aid of the Palmetto State when she took the final step.

However, Georgia moved so rapidly that he found there the opportunity he was seeking. As a lieutenant colonel in command of the Twenty-sixth Regiment, Georgia Infantry, Lamar hoped to take the initiative by attacking a federal installation; but Governor Joseph E. Brown bypassed the slave trader. Months before the official start of the Civil War at Fort Sumter, Brown ordered Colonel Alexander R. Lawton of the First Regiment, Georgia Volunteers, to seize Fort Pulaski at the mouth of the Savannah River.

Lamar was ordered to take charge of the defense of Jekyll Island. Chagrined at being so far removed from battle, he gave up his commission and resumed his shipping business.

However, as the war neared its end, he offered his services to the Georgia home guard commanded by General Howell Cobb. Of the decimated Confederate forces, this was all that was left to defend the state.

Thus Charles Augustus Lafayette Lamar found himself near the Chattahoochee River on Easter Sunday, 1865, with a small body of state troops that he hoped would thwart a cavalry raid of Federal General James H. Wilson.

Captured unarmed about sundown on April 16, Lamar was shot when men in blue thought he was reaching for a gun. As a result, the nation's last operator of a slave ship is frequently listed as the last combat casualty of the Civil War.

21

Runaway Thomas Sims Helped Shape the Nation's Destiny

"Sumner Sure to Make His Mark in Washington," read newspaper headlines. Though not identical in language, that prediction appeared on the front page of every Boston daily in July, 1851.

Fiery Charles Sumner, who stood an imposing six-feet, four-inches tall, intended to live up to expectations. In an Independence Day speech, he thanked his supporters. "Most of all," he said, "I am forever grateful to Thomas Sims."

Listeners and newspaper readers applauded that sentiment because no one present during those days of tumult would ever forget the runaway from Georgia.

Despite his potent influence, little is known about Sims's background. No standard history of the state, not even a multivolume set, mentions his name, because Sims was a slave. Not an ordinary, run-of-the-mill slave, he was a cunning, courageous, and altogether defiant seventeen-year-old who chose George Washington's birthday in 1851 as the day for making his getaway.

However, within sixty days, Sims was wearing handcuffs and leg irons in Boston, "the cradle of American liberty." There police had seized him under provisions of the 1850 Fugitive Slave Law. He'd been in the port city for a month, not bothering to hide as he thought he had nothing to fear while within earshot of battlefields where men had died in the name of freedom.

Since Sims was the legal property of Georgia planter James Potter, the law required that he be returned to Georgia and slavery by the first available vessel.

However, abolitionist sympathy was strong in Boston. Richard H. Dana, Jr., and Samuel E. Sewall volunteered their services as attorneys for the defense, as did attorney Charles Sumner, still smarting from his unsuccessful bid for a seat in the U.S. House of Representatives but now being

Boston police, 300 strong, escort Sims to ship.

mentioned as a possible candidate for the U.S. Senate. Although this high-powered defense team was unable to change the law, it could create a public furor. Posters were printed, warning "colored people of Boston" to avoid contact with police officers. Wendell Phillips and William Lloyd Garrison put their tremendous influence behind an organized effort to save Sims from deportation.

Military units were assigned to guard the courthouse where Sims was being held. Boston churches held special prayer meetings; street orators harangued excited crowds.

In an effort to prevent mayhem, authorities ringed the courthouse with a heavy chain. A pack of bloodhounds was held in readiness, and three hundred special policemen were sworn in to guard the prisoner.

Rumors spread like wildfire. Two hundred men from Worcester and another one hundred from Plymouth County were said to be preparing to descend on the port city armed with muskets to effect forcible rescue of Thomas Sims.

Although these armed bands never appeared, Marshal Tukey assembled all three hundred special police officers about 4:00 A.M. on Saturday, April 13, and hustled Sims out of his improvised cell.

Captive and captors marched through Court Square, crossed the spot where the first American freedom fighter had died in the Boston Massacre of 1770, and boarded the *Acorn*. Sims was locked up in a specially built shed and sent to Savannah, where he was publicly whipped upon arrival.

The first person ever returned to slavery from Massachusetts soil, he was heard from no more after his return to the Georgia plantation. However, he was not forgotten, and his *cause célèbre* had far-reaching repercussions.

In Massachusetts, Sumner, Phillips, and Dana repeatedly invoked the slave's name. Although they failed in their immediate goal of repealing the Fugitive Slave Law, they aroused the common people mightily.

*Georgia fugitive
Thomas Sims.*

Members of the state legislature heard the roar of the people and voted to send Charles Sumner to the U.S. Senate. There the man who owed his seat to publicity about a runaway slave became chief architect of a plan that called for emancipation, even at the cost of blood. His ardent speeches in support of that hard-line, no-compromise plan made Sims's defender a prime mover in bringing about the Civil War.

22

Georgia Home of Songwriter
Was a Log Jail

John Howard Payne, who wrote the lyrics of "Home, Sweet Home," came to Georgia in 1835, but he found no homelike atmosphere here. Certainly his stay in the state could not be described as "sweet" in any way.

A native New Yorker, he displayed creativity very early in life. At thirteen he published a magazine, then became an actor and playwright. During an interlude in Europe, a song from an opera he adapted from one of his plays became "Home, Sweet Home," but his theatrical ventures proved unsuccessful and he was imprisoned for debt.

Once he was back in America, although friends called him "an impractical dreamer of grandiloquent schemes," he vowed to publish and edit the finest magazine the world had yet seen. His proposed brain-child would contain both literary and scientific articles, for which subscribers would pay ten dollars a year, an unusually high rate for the time. It would bear no title except a phrase *Jam Jehan Nima*, signifying a legendary oriental cup, or "the bowl in which you may see the universe."

Since Payne planned to be his own chief writer, he announced a beginning publication date far in the future to give him time to gather the information first-hand.

Seeking material, he traveled down the Mississippi River by flatboat to New Orleans. Then he turned east to become acquainted with Indians and to make notes about their customs.

At the Creek village of Tuckabatchie, the wandering idealist saw the Dance of the Green Corn, so powerful in its emotional effect that he confessed himself "practically intoxicated" by it.

His interest in Indians having been raised to a new level, he inquired about other places to find good material and was told that North Georgia was the place to go. Here the Cherokees were known to have developed an elaborate culture. To make things more interesting, they were then central actors in a national drama.

Twenty-five years earlier, Georgia had ceded her western territory to the nation, and in return expected all Indians to be removed from its lands. However, when Payne reached the region, native Americans still held ten million acres of Georgia land.

If Washington would not act, Milledgeville could and would. From the state capital, survey crews were sent to lay out the entire Indian domain into ten counties. Then the land would be assigned to whites through a series of lotteries.

Into this volatile situation Payne arrived in Macon in August, 1835, where he wrote a letter to his sister describing his feelings as a spectator at the Dance of the Green Corn. "It was a melancholy reflection," he wrote, "to know that these strange people were rapidly becoming extinct, along with their folklore—which would perhaps unfold to man the most remarkable of all human histories."

Then prodding his horse to move as fast as possible, the writer pushed north into Cherokee country to launch the ambitious project of recording and thus preserving all Cherokee lore.

In the process Payne formed a friendship with John Ross, a Cherokee chief who was fighting to preserve his tribe's homeland. On November 7, both he and John Ross were arrested by members of the Georgia Guard. Headed toward

John Howard Payne.

jail, Payne heard one of his captors humming "Home, Sweet Home." That gave him an opportunity to introduce himself as author of the song and to comment that "the circumstances under which I now hear these words strike me as rather singular."

Song or no song, the outsider was a meddler, aiding and abetting the Indians in obstructing Georgia's plans to seize total possession of all disputed lands. So he was put in a log jail with no sanitary facilities. Rough mattresses were stuffed with corn shucks; vermin abounded on the dirt floor, and prison food was sparse and poorly prepared.

Although Payne at first vowed to stay in jail forever, if necessary, he soon contacted influential friends who secured his release after just twelve days. A condition of his release was that he leave the state and never return.

All of his precious papers and notes had been seized, so he had only memories from which to prepare material for the splendid magazine he still hoped to launch.

From Georgia, Payne rode to Knoxville where he talked angrily of the jail that had constituted his most memorable Georgia abode. Then he published a blistering "Address to Fellow Countrymen," in which he vowed he'd never again enter Georgia without a formal invitation.

He never got that invitation. A few years later he became U.S. Consul at Tunis, Tunisia, where he died far away, indeed, from his home, sweet home.

23

Vice-President Aaron Burr Hid from the Law on St. Simons

The coattails of history have brushed Georgia's Sea Islands many times. There pirates are said to have buried their loot; John and Charles Wesley, founders of Methodism, preached under their ancient oak trees; and Vice-President Aaron Burr took refuge on St. Simons after his duel with Alexander Hamilton.

Burr is thought to have chosen his hide-out partly because of its seclusion but mainly because it belonged to his long-time wealthy friend, Pierce Butler of South Carolina. A delegate to the Constitutional Convention and then a five-term congressman, Butler retired from public life in 1803. Owning fifteen thousand acres in Georgia, he chose to live at Hampton Point, his "principal residence" on St. Simons Island that was described as being "of feudal magnificence."

From there, the fugitive Burr wrote to his daughter:

I am at the mansion of Major Butler, and am most comfortably settled. My personal establishment consists of a housekeeper, a cook and chambermaid, a seamstress, and two footmen. In addition, I always have two fishermen and four boatmen at my command.

How Burr came to be Butler's "guest" on St. Simons is a sad story in American history.

His background included service on Washington's staff in the Revolution, a term in the U.S. Senate, and then the presidential campaigns of 1796 and 1800. He lost the first election but tied with Thomas Jefferson in the second. Under the Constitution at that time, the winner would be president, while the second vote-gatherer would be vice-president, with the House of Representatives determining the outcome. Alexander Hamilton, brilliant author of the *Federalist* papers and the first secretary of the treasury, used his influence to give victory to Jefferson, thereby incurring Burr's enmity.

Vice-President Burr then ran for governor of New York in 1804 but was defeated. Again Burr felt that Hamilton had been instrumental in his loss.

Just before the election, Dr. Charles D. Cooper had written an open letter published in several newspapers. Hamilton, who had opposed Burr zealously, was mentioned in the letters, although he had not seen the document, and had nothing to do with its circulation.

Nevertheless Burr demanded a public apology from Hamilton, who refused. They exchanged several brief messages through intermediaries, but the notes created an increasingly tense situation. Eventually Burr challenged Hamilton to a duel, and Hamilton accepted immediately, asking only that he be given time to take care of a few personal and legal matters.

Their seconds attended to the details. Burr and Hamilton met at Weehawken, New Jersey, on July 11, 1804.

Both men drew up and signed wills. Burr placed his affairs in the hands of his daughter Theodosia, pointing out that his estate would only cover his debts. Hamilton wrote a long summary of his thoughts and stressed that he bore Burr no ill will.

Wednesday, July 11, dawned hot and muggy as the seconds preceded the principals to a narrow ledge overlooking the Hudson River. There they cleared sticks and stones from the area.

The elaborate ritual began promptly at 7:00 A.M. The seconds counted off ten paces, then cast lots to determine positions and selected the one who would give the commands. Then they loaded the pistols. Hamilton had borrowed his from his brother-in-law, John B. Church.

Upon command, both men fired. Hamilton's shot went wild and snapped a small limb of a tree, but Burr's ball hit Hamilton in the abdomen. He died at 2:00 P.M. on July 12.

Though the duel took place in New Jersey, a New York coroner's jury indicted Burr for murder. When a warrant was issued for his arrest, he fled, taking along his friend, Samuel Swartwout, and his favorite slave.

Hiding briefly in Philadelphia, they then travelled in disguise to Georgia, conveniently close to Spanish Florida. By now also indicted in New Jersey, Burr used the name Mr. R. King, but dropped pretense soon after reaching St. Simons. There he was "serenaded by the island's only band of music."

Burr's Georgia stay was punctuated by a hurricane, but he stayed until time for Congress to convene again. On February 4, 1805, Vice President Aaron Burr—still under indictment for murder—took his seat to preside over the United States Senate until his term ended.

His career did not end there, of course. Politically ruined, he engaged in questionable activities in the West and was tried for treason in 1807 at a trial presided over by Supreme Court Chief Justice John Marshall. Burr was acquitted and went to Europe, returning to practice law in New York City.

However, his sojourn on St. Simons adds another chapter to the exciting tales of Georgia's Sea Islands.

24

Claiming Innocence, Swiss Doctor Died for War Crimes

"I am innocent," the prisoner said to the soldiers who were busy preparing him for execution.

Calmly, almost dispassionately—in contrast to earlier shouts and pleas—Henri Wirz seemed to be choosing his words carefully. Minutes earlier, as his hands were being tied, he had refused the offer of Catholic priests Boyle and Wiggett to hear his confession. Not being guilty, he told them, he had nothing to confess.

With only General John Winder and a few others present to hear it, the Swiss-born Confederate officer entered his last plea, addressed, not to them, but to the court of final appeal.

"I go before my God, the Almighty God who will judge us all," he said. "I will die like a man. I pray that then I may be found without guilt—simply a soldier who has always obeyed his orders."

Minutes later, at 10:15 A.M. on November 10, 1885, the former commandant of Andersonville prison downed half a bottle of whisky. Wincing from the constant pain of a shoulder wound that had never healed, made worse by surgery in Paris, he made the sign of the cross, then walked calmly across the courtyard of Washington's Old Capitol prison.

Earlier the spot had become famous as the place where the conspirators convicted of President Lincoln's murder had been executed. Now it was about to gain more notoriety, to be remembered as having held the scaffold on which the only "war criminal" of the Civil War was executed.

Since only 250 cards had been distributed for spectators' seats, hundreds more contested for good spots in elm trees surrounding the courtyard. Newspaper correspondents, wearing top hats, were ushered to a reserved section.

As the doomed man mounted the scaffold, onlookers in trees shouted curses. Soldiers, standing at attention, began to chant:

"Wirz! Wirz! Remember Andersonville! Wirz! Wirz! Remember Andersonville!"

"Thank you for the courtesy you have shown me," said the man born Heinrich Hartmann Wirz to his jailers as he left the cell he had occupied during his three-month trial.

With eyes open, he climbed the scaffold, then stood stiffly while a black hood was slipped over his head. A veteran executioner applied the noose and adjusted it.

At the touch of a spring, the trap door opened, and Wirz plunged; but the fall failed to snap his neck. As he slowly strangled, the only sounds came from men in blue still chanting, "Wirz! Wirz! Remember Andersonville!"

Alexander Gardner, a photographer with the studio of Mathew Brady, captured the entire drama in a series of vivid shots.

The chain of events leading to this fatal day caused the presiding judge at Wirz's trial, General Lew Wallace, who later wrote the novel *Ben Hur*, to characterize the accused as "an immigrant who became a rebel almost by accident."

Though he claimed to be a physician, Wirz had no formal medical training. Some time early in the 1850s the man who had come to America seeking opportunity became an assistant to a Kentucky doctor. When efforts to establish his own practice failed, he drifted to Louisiana and took a job on a plantation. Listed as "Dr. Wirz," he may have been employed to care for sick and injured slaves.

When the Civil War started, he enlisted in the Fourth Louisiana Infantry, where he soon rose to the rank of ser-

Execution of Capt. Henri Wirz.

geant. At Seven Pines he took a ball in his shoulder and permanently lost the use of his right hand and arm. Partly to compensate him for his injury, he was promoted to the rank of captain.

Brigadier General John Winder liked the man whom many still called the "Dutch sergeant" even after he rose in rank. As provost marshall in Richmond, Winder was in charge of Confederate prisons in the capital city. Since Wirz was known to be "the epitome of military obedience," Winder made him commandant of a prison.

Wirz performed his duties so well—never asking questions of superiors—that Jefferson Davis sent him on a mission to Paris. While he was there surgeons tried to restore his right arm to usefulness, but they failed.

Back in the Confederate States of America, the self-trained doctor was sent to Georgia's Andersonville prison in March, 1864.

There he found food and water critically low. Prisoners soon began to fight over scraps of bread and the bodies of dead rats. They died by the dozen, then by the score, and finally by the hundred—every day of every week.

The situation became much worse when General Ulysses Grant gave the prison his personal attention. Tens of thousands of men who fought in blue had enlisted for limited terms, and for many who languished in Confederate prisons such as Andersonville, the calendar offered a new life. Their enlistments had expired, or were about to expire. Upon being exchanged, they could put on civilian clothes and turn their backs upon the war.

Therefore, Grant's decision was logical from the standpoint of military strategy, but totally heartless from the perspective of prisoners. He put an abrupt halt to the exchange of prisoners, thereby shrinking the available pool of potential Confederate soldiers that was desperately needed by the hard-pressed South.

More and more captured men were crowed into Confederate prisons with no possibility of relief through exchange. By July, 1864, about 32,000 men were jammed into twenty-six acres of shanties. There were no sanitary facilities, little medicine, and less food. More than 12,900 prisoners died.

Collapse of the Confederate States of America was followed by a national outpouring of indignation about conditions in "the notorious Hell Hole" commanded by Captain Henri Wirz. He was seized and charged with mass murder. After his condemnation, he was offered a reprieve in return for a statement that would make Jefferson Davis guilty of having conspired to murder prisoners.

"No, no," Wirz said. "He did not do it. You cannot make me say that he did." Having turned down a chance to save his own life, the man who had obeyed orders went to the scaffold.

25

Manhunt Netted President Jefferson Davis

"Somebody belonging to the Fourth Michigan Cavalry fired the first shot," insisted Lieutenant Colonel Henry Harnden of the First Wisconsin Cavalry.

"Not on your life!" retorted Lieutenant Colonel B. D. Pritchard. "My men responded when shots were fired at us. We thought we had contacted a rebel unit and had no idea that the First Wisconsin was trying to grab our prize."

These conflicting statements—never fully resolved— came on the heels of the capture of Jefferson Davis, President of the Confederate States of America. For days, he had been the object of a manhunt until pursuers caught up with him in a dense thicket about two miles from Irwinville, Georgia, on May 16, 1865.

Federal authorities, who wanted to bring Davis to trial on a charge of high treason, were frenzied with fear that he might escape. That led to a colossal offer: $100,000 in gold for his capture.

Bounty hunters, plus two military units, followed Davis's trail through parts of the Carolinas and into Georgia. Both the Michigan and the Wisconsin units were close to claiming the reward on the night of May 9. Before dawn, each group moved forward. A fusillade between the two Federal bodies led to at least one death plus several injuries. The ludicrous aspects of the miniature battle were forgotten

Jefferson Davis.

when the fugitive was captured one week later, with official credit going to the Fourth Michigan Cavalry.

The drama began on a quiet Sunday morning, April 2. While worshiping in Saint Paul's church in Richmond, Jefferson Davis received a hand-delivered telegram.

General Robert E. Lee, who had sent the message, warned that Richmond would soon fall and urged immediate evacuation of the Confederate capital. Many people fled during the next twenty-four hours. Three groups are vividly remembered.

Mrs. Jefferson Davis, with her four children and a small band of escorts, made up the first such party, heading south with only vague plans about their final destination.

On the evening of April 2, a larger group left the city with an armed escort guarding a wagon train carrying what was left of the Confederate treasury, plus assets of several Virginia banks.

A third refugee party was headed by Confederate President Jefferson Davis. Not yet aware of the price put on his head, the Confederate chief executive hoped to make his way across the Mississippi to Louisiana. If he could reach the Trans-Mississippi Department of the Confederate army, he thought he could rally the remaining soldiers and perhaps bargain for re-admission of the southern states to the union on favorable terms.

Members of Davis's cabinet were told to meet in Washington, Georgia, although no arrival date was set.

Dotted line shows route of Davis's flight.

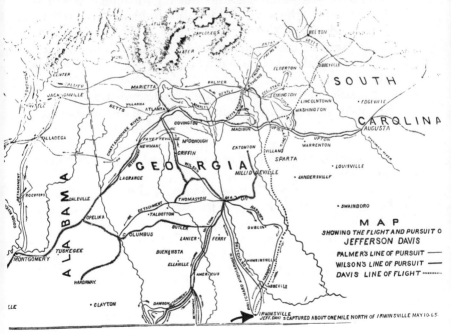

Traveling mostly at night, the fleeing president and his party reached Washington on May 4. The town had been selected as the rendezvous spot partly because it was the home of Confederate General Robert Toombs and partly because it was thought to be safely within Confederate territory.

On the night he reached Washington, Davis signed his last official order, naming M. H. Clark as acting treasurer of the Confederate States of America and giving him a free hand to exercise his office. Clark immediately took charge of the five heavily loaded wagons and headed in the direction of Abbeville, South Carolina.

No one knows how much gold and silver the wagons held, but estimates range from about $250,000 to more than $400,000, with some accounts placing the total at ten times that estimate. However, unidentified raiders surprised the driver and guards on the night of May 5. They seized some of the precious metal and are said to have sunk more of it in the Savannah River or buried it on a Wilkes County, Georgia, plantation.

Unaware of the loss of the Confederate treasury, Davis and his party slowly moved southward, where they managed to meet Mrs. Davis and her party near Dublin on May 7. Continuing to move forward cautiously, they sometimes traveled only eight to ten miles a day until Federal units finally found and captured them.

Sent to Virginia's Fortress Monroe and clapped in irons, Davis stayed in confinement for two years. Never brought to trial, he was released on May 13, 1867, on a $100,000 bail bond whose co-signers included Cornelius Vanderbilt and professional South-hater Horace Greeley. Charges against him were dropped in 1868.

PART FIVE:
Original Americans

26

First Land Pirate Was an Indian Princess

"It was Coosaponakessa's land, and her labor that produced the first crop of wheat for the colony you call Savannah," read one clause of a lengthy legal document.

"Coosaponakessa is not greedy. Fifty pounds will be enough for this," the itemized list of claims continued.

Using her native name, the woman whom James Oglethorpe knew as Mary Musgrove enumerated the services for which she had not been paid.

While Europeans had failed in attempts to grow peas and potatoes, she pointed out, she had succeeded grandly. Still she'd settle for just 150 pounds. Another claim was much larger. She had been promised 100 pounds per year for service as interpreter to James Oglethorpe and his aides and had filled the post for many years.

Half Indian and half English, Mary was listed in numerous early Georgia documents as "Empress and Queen of the Upper and Lower Creeks." Her title derived from the fact that Old Brim, a noted chieftain, was her uncle. After her marriage to a Carolina-born trader John Musgrove, she helped him operate a trading post at Yamacraw village, not far from the site selected for Savannah. She claimed to have been handling 1,200 deerskins a year when Oglethorpe and his followers arrived from England and immediately hired her as his interpreter. The pay was unusually large for the time.

Another Englishman also thought highly of her. Missionary John Wesley was delighted to learn that the wife of trader John Musgrove was a Christian.

After visiting Mary at her plantation about six miles up the Savannah river from her trading post, Wesley wrote in his diary that she was the most capable "native Georgian ever encountered while in the colony."

When Oglethorpe needed undercover agents, he turned to the Musgroves who went into "the debatable land" that was claimed by Britain, Spain, and France. There they established Mount Venture, a trading post about 150 miles above the mouth of the Altamaha River. Close to the Spanish territory of Florida, it was an ideal site from which to spy upon the vital overland trail that linked Charles Town with Saint Augustine.

When John Musgrove died, Mary married Jacob Matthews, who had come to the colony as an indentured servant. As husband of an Indian princess "he grew vain, dressing gaily and behaving insolently." However, he played

Oglethorpe addresses native Georgians through female interpreter.

The Rev. *John Wesley seeks converts at Musgrove's trading post.*

the role of prince only a few months before he died in 1742.

Soon afterwards Oglethorpe prepared to return to England. One of his last acts was to take a diamond ring from his own finger and to place it upon the finger of his interpreter. At the same time he is said to have given her 200 pounds of his own money and the promise to send 2,000 more pounds when he arrived home.

Mary then married the Reverend Thomas Bosomworth. As the first native American to become the wife of an Anglican priest, she took no part in his official duties as chaplain to the infant colony and trading post enterprise. She was busy selling illicit rum at high prices. She also busily amassed land grants from various Indian chieftains, both Creek and Yamacraw. However, authorities in London refused to honor the claims based on land transactions among the Indians. To get firm title to her holdings, plus payment in cash for services rendered in the past, Coosaponakessa had to persuade

British authorities to rule in her favor. Her initial request stipulated that she would withdraw from legal action in return for cash payment of 5,714 pounds, 17 shillings, and 11 pence, plus deeds to the islands of Hussoope (Ossabaw), Cowlegee (Saint Catherine's), and Sapelo.

The trustees of the Georgia colony in London stalled her, then eventually decided they didn't have authority to act. So the matter went to the Board of Trade. Month after month passed with no action there.

Angry and determined, Coosaponakessa and her husband sailed to England to present her claims in person. Official bodies shunted them from one to another, pointing out that no native American had ever presented such demands to the home government.

Thwarted but determined not to be defeated, the Bosomworths returned to Savannah and adroitly timed the next move.

Succeeding John Reynolds, first royal governor of Georgia, was Henry Ellis, a man with little administrative experience. Coosaponakessa thereupon recruited a band of Indian followers and invaded Savannah, threatening to launch all-out war against the white settlers unless her claims were settled.

Bewildered and frightened, Ellis convened the colonial council, which decided "to bargain for the sake of peace" and offered their challenger 2,100 pounds, sterling, plus Saint Catherine's Island.

Without consulting her husband other than by brief gestures, the Indian princess accepted their offer and formally released Great Britain from all other claims. Then she took possession of her island, built a splendid mansion and developed a fine plantation.

No other native American ever turned the tables so completely on colonial officialdom, wresting land *from* the British, as did Coosaponakessa. This "Queen of the Creeks" lived happily ever after as a true New World queen.

27

Chimneys Cracked in Athens When Shawnee Chief Stamped His Foot

"Your blood is white!" shouted Tecumseh, enraged that Big Warrior had refused to join in a ceremonial dance.

"You do not believe the Great Spirit has sent me," he charged. "You shall know! I leave you now. But when I am back at the Tippecanoe, I will stamp on the ground with my foot and will shake every house in Tuckabatchee!"

Son of Methoatagke, a native of Georgia, and the Shawnee chief Puckeshinwa, Tecumseh was born in the Scioto River Valley of Ohio. When his father and two brothers were killed by American colonists, the adolescent boy persuaded his people to retaliate. They captured twenty-seven whites. One of them, Daniel Boone, managed to escape, but most were killed and scalped.

A strong warrior and gifted orator, Tecumseh became a leading spokesman for all native Americans in a crusade to keep Indian lands for the Indians. As an advocate of a confederation of all North American Indians, he traveled from his home in Ohio to almost every tribe east of the Rocky Mountains, telling them they could defeat the white man.

"Give up no more land," he urged constantly. "It is ours. Our ancestors wail with the winds every time we let the white man move farther into our territory."

Under Tecumseh's urging, many western tribes united, but they were not strong enough to fight an all-out war.

Tecumseh.

Therefore the Indian leader made a long journey to the South in 1811. Victory was almost certain, he believed, if he could persuade warriors of Florida, Georgia, Alabama, North Carolina, and Tennessee to join the confederation.

In Florida, he got half-hearted promises. Creeks from South Georgia told him they were willing to fight, but only if many other tribes gave the same pledge.

It was in this climate that the Indian with Georgia roots headed toward the annual grand council of the Muskogees, which convened at Tuckabatchee on the Tallapoosa River, close to present-day Montgomery, Alabama. In ordinary years 5000 warriors usually gathered for the October conclave; more would be there in 1811 to ponder the proposals brought by the Shawnee.

For the ceremonial meeting with Big Warrior, head of the Muskogees, Tecumseh and his twenty-four braves wore war paint and bonnets. One white man, General Sam Dale, watched, listened, and recorded his impressions of the pow-wow.

Speaking for all of the Creeks, Big Warrior asked for time before deciding whether to go to war. His equivocation enraged Tecumseh, who let out "a most diabolical yell." Then he scattered tobacco and sumac to purify the ground and drive away evil spirits.

Unable to prod Big Warrior into decisive action, Tecumseh uttered his fearful warning, then left to enlist the Cherokees in the coming war.

Some of Big Warrior's medicine men took Tecumseh seriously enough to mark off the days. Had they been using the white man's calendar, the threatened time of destruction would have been about the middle of December.

Meanwhile, in November, Tecumseh met General William Henry Harrison at the Battle of Tippecanoe and was defeated.

Then on December 16, 1811, citizens throughout the entire Southland awoke to strange goings on. Folks in Athens, Georgia, felt as though they were aboard a ship; in Augusta, dishes rattled; in Tuckabatchee, some people thought their walls were going to tumble down; and far to the west, the mighty Mississippi flowed backward. An earthquake centered at New Madrid, Missouri, equal to ten on the modern Richter scale, had caused the earth to tremble and houses to collapse even as Tecumseh had prophesied.

Taking this cataclysmic event as approbation from the Great Spirit for his cause, Tecumseh joined with the British in the War of 1812. As a brigadier general in command of England's Indian allies, "the warrior who stamped his foot to make the earth shake" was killed in action in Canada.

However, the "footprint" of this son of a Georgia woman can still be seen today: Reelfoot Lake in Tennessee was formed by the gigantic earthquake of 1811.

28

Alexander McGillivray Got Even with Georgia

No other British colony in North America equaled Georgia in her loyalty to the mother country. When the American Revolution began, the colony was young and still very, very British.

Patriots had to leave the region or go into hiding during long periods of British occupation, but after Yorktown they had a splendid opportunity, on which they acted with zeal. Once they were in control of the state, they passed legislation under which property of Tories was confiscated, and many wealthy people were ruined.

One who lost all of his Georgia holdings was Lachlan McGillivray, a redheaded, blue-eyed Scot who had become a prosperous trader with the Indians. Moving into what is now Alabama, he had settled at Little Tallassie on the Tallapoosa River and had quadrupled his wealth in a few years. Much of his profit went into Georgia real estate.

McGillivray's wife was Sehoy of the Tribe of the Wind, whose French father had married a high-born Creek woman. Their son was named Alexander, of whom an early biographer wrote, "He possesses the polished urbanity of the Frenchman, the cool sagacity of the Scotchman, and the silent subtlety and inveterate hate of the North American Indian."

Alexander's hate stemmed, according to him, from anger

at the unjust way in which Georgia confiscated his father's holdings. He swore that he'd get even, if it took him a lifetime to do so.

Much of his boyhood had been spent in Charleston, where he studied under a Scots-Presbyterian relative. Later he worked for a time in Savannah. He was a linguist, and had a good education in the classics. Yet to all whites—and to himself—he was an Indian.

When Georgia seized the McGillivray property, Alexander took refuge at Little Tallassie, where his mother's people, he reasoned, could help him to get revenge against Georgia. At the death of the Cherokee ruler Oconostota, the man with the blood of three nations in his veins seized power, eventually dominating a large Indian confederacy that included Creeks, Seminoles, and Cherokees. At the height of his power, Alexander McGillivray could have put ten thousand warriors into the field.

Adroitly dealing with representatives of Spain, England, and the new United States, the Indian leader deftly played

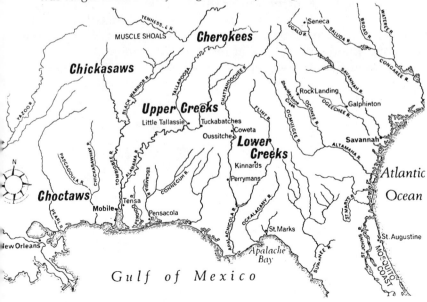

From Little Tallassie, Alexander McGillivray's domain was larger than that of the governor of Georgia.

each against the others to achieve his goal of moving the American boundary back to its 1773 lines. Thus he, as a large land owner in Indian territory, would control almost all of present-day Alabama and Mississippi.

From his numerous "palaces" in the land of the Upper Creeks, McGillivray dickered with both England and Spain, until George Washington himself asked him to come to the capital in New York to discuss the situation. There he became an instant celebrity. Mrs. John Adams, who entertained him, confided in her diary that the man from the southwestern frontier "behaved with much civility."

Eventually he finagled a large cash settlement and received from President Washington a commission in the U.S. Army, with a guaranteed annual salary. Apparently it made no difference that he was already a British colonel and a Spanish general, and he managed simultaneously to draw pay from the militaries of three nations.

No warrior himself, McGillivray left the fighting to others, preferring to attain his goals by scheming. Admirers compared him with the French master of intrigue, calling him "an American Talleyrand."

Although Georgia had stripped him of his inheritance, at the height of his power he ruled a domain larger than the state of Georgia. When he died in 1793, McGillivray left three large plantations and at least sixty slaves. Yet today no one knows what this shrewd, rich, and powerful man looked like. He refused to allow his portrait to be painted.

29

Last Confederate General to Surrender Was Stand Watie

Lee's surrender at Appomattox on April 12, 1865, is generally considered to have concluded the Civil War.

Not so. Here is the end of the story.

A little-known Georgia native led his men into the Oklahoma brush and dared Union forces to follow him. From the saddles of a few of the Confederates led by Brigadier General Stand Watie dangled scalps of Union soldiers.

Riding by night and hiding by day, Watie and his men eluded numerically superior Federal units for ten weeks after Appomattox.

Doaksville, near Fort Towson in the Indian Territory, saw the finish. There General Watie, picturesque black hair falling to his shoulders, surrendered to Colonel Asa Mathews. It was the last formal submission of any significant body of Rebels, and the last surrender of a Confederate general.

Watie was no newcomer to war. In 1837 he was a leader of the tribal faction that signed the Treaty of New Echota. Under its terms, Georgia's Cherokees agreed to move to the West.

Preferring to fight, rather than leave ancestral lands, most of the Cherokees believed that the $5 million payment promised in the treaty would go into the pockets of Major Ridge, his son John, Elias Boudinot, and Stand Watie.

However, Federal troops forced them to follow the "Trail of

Tears" to Oklahoma. There embittered tribesmen murdered most of the leaders of the faction that had assented to the treaty, but Stand Watie escaped the vengeance of his fellow braves.

Nearly a quarter of a century later, the Georgia native was approached by Massachusetts-born Albert Pike, then living in Little Rock, Arkansas. Confederate authorities had given Pike a general's commission, plus a free hand to try to persuade the Indians of the West to become allies of the confederacy.

*Brigadier-general Albert Pike
recruited Indians for the Confederate
States of America.*

To accomplish this, Pike drew up a new and different kind of treaty in August of 1861.

In return for military assistance, he promised to provide tribesmen with sugar, coffee, salt, soap, vinegar, and forty cows and calves plus one bull for every one hundred persons. There was also an ironclad guarantee that native Americans who had been driven from the East would be given their own state, once the Yankees capitulated. Comaches, Shawnees, and Delawares signed the treaty, followed closely by Cherokees.

Altogether, an estimated 5,500 men enlisted in Pike's three Indian brigades, but only one unit fought on the Union side. Stand Watie, and most Cherokee warriors who had opposed the treaty of New Echota, fought for the Confederacy.

The biggest engagement in which Watie's troops took part was called Pea Ridge by Yankees and Elkhorn Tavern by Confederates. Here in March, 1862, 12,000 men in blue secured Missouri for the Union by defeating 16,000 men in gray at this site. Losses were heavy on both sides, with Samuel Curtis, the Union commander, reporting ten percent of his men killed.

When the war ended, the Federal government exacted a heavy toll against the Cherokees and other members of the Five Civilized Tribes. For having made a military alliance with the Confederate States of America, these native Americans were forced to cede to the U.S. government the western half of lands they had received at the end of the Trail of Tears.

30

Half-White Framed a Treaty That Became His Death Warrant

"Brothers you are being deceived! A snake has been coiled in the shade. You are running in his mouth, deceived by the double tongue of the paleface chief, McIntosh! You are drunk with the firewater of the paleface!"

Pausing in his rhythmic chant, Ho-po-eth-le-yo-ho-lo strutted through a few steps of a ritualistic war dance. Then he turned to half-breed William McIntosh, who was leader of the Lower Creeks and was an outspoken advocate of a new treaty that required surrender of yet more land.

"As for you, double-tongued snake," chanted the Upper Creek leader, "before many moons have waned your own blood will wash out the memory of this hated treaty! Brothers, I have spoken!"

Followed by thirty-five other braves, the spokesman of Alabama's Red Sticks, or Upper Creeks, left the conference at Warm Springs, Georgia, and returned home.

With only a half-dozen minor Indian leaders supporting him, General William McIntosh bargained and haggled for five more days. Then on February 12, 1825, he signed the treaty giving Georgia possession of all remaining Creek lands in the state. The area of the cession was about four times that of the land occupied by whites during the leadership of James Oglethorpe.

Exactly what McIntosh got for the sellout of his people is

not known, but some records suggest that his personal 640-acre tract brought him $25,000, an immense sum for the time.

Born at Coweta, Georgia, in 1775, McIntosh was the son of a British army officer and a Creek mother. His father's sister, Catherine, was mother of Georgia Governor George M. Troup. Very early, McIntosh revealed his willingness to cooperate with his cousin George and other whites. Bad blood between the Lower Creeks of Georgia and the Red Sticks of Alabama made this easy.

Red Sticks, or Upper Creeks, were allies of the British during the War of 1812 when William McIntosh led his Lower Creeks into battle against them. At Horseshoe Bend, Alabama, his 700 warriors tipped the balance in favor of forces commanded by General Andrew Jackson.

An estimated 500 Upper Creeks died in the battle on March 29, 1814, and many are believed to have been slaughtered in cold blood after having attempted to surrender. As a result, McIntosh was promoted to brigadier general and the Red Sticks became his implacable foes.

That is one of many reasons they refused to sign the Treaty of Indian Springs. Under its terms, McIntosh and his followers were to move west of the Mississippi within twelve months where they would receive new tribal land, plus $400,000 in cash.

In the region that later became Tallapoosa County, Alabama, the Red Sticks made careful plans. Waiting until spring floods made it difficult for troops of the Georgia militia to cross swollen rivers, they set out by night for the man who had made a bargain with the whites.

When discovered by settlers about 1792, Indian Springs was already noted for its medicinal waters. Here, William McIntosh built one of his homes about 1800. He spent much of his time there, but also visited his two Cherokee wives at his Carroll County plantation. He rarely saw his white wife, Eliza, who managed his place on the Tallapoosa River.

McIntosh was fully aware of the law passed by a Creek conclave at Pole Cat Springs condemning any Indian who tried to give away tribal lands to "death by rope and by gun." So he was not surprised when the war party arrived during the night of April 29, 1825.

As soon as he heard his enemies, McIntosh withdrew with four rifles to the second story of his home on the Chattahoochee. His foes gathered fat pine and put the house he called Lockchau Talofau to the torch.

No one could hold out against at least 170 attackers. McIntosh was felled by a hunting knife, then each Red Stick warrior was allowed to fire a shot into his body. Afterward he was scalped and the war trophy was taken to Ocfuskee, Alabama, and suspended on a pole.

Early Georgia historians unanimously lauded General William McIntosh as "a devoted friend of the American people." In 1911, a chapter of the Daughters of American Revolution erected a memorial tablet praising the half-breed who sold out the Creeks. It failed to note that his "savage murder" came about precisely as Ho-po-eth-le-yo-ho-lo had threatened when he warned against yielding land to the white man.

31

Congressman's Protege Chose to Live as a Cherokee

"I trust that the Cherokees will be admitted into all the privileges of the American family. Polygamy is abolished. Female chastity and honor are protected by law. Murder has become a governmental crime."

Worshipers in the First Presbyterian Church of Philadelphia, Pennsylvania, nodded their gratification, as Georgia-born Elias Boudinot, guest speaker, then turned to his central theme.

"Cherokees have thought it advisable that they should have a printing press," he said. When before did a nation of Indians step forward and ask for the means of civilization?

"I can view my native country taking her seat with the nations of earth. Like the first morning sun, she is now growing brighter hour by hour!"

Many whites who listened made contributions to the fund that had been established in Boston to provide Cherokees of faraway Georgia with equipment to begin printing in their own language. Some worshipers—a minority—bristled, whispered to one another, and shook their heads when the collection plate came to them. They were convinced that the speaker was headed for trouble.

The speaker, Buck Oowaytee, was born in the Oothcaloga Valley of Georgia in 1804, so he was just twenty-two when he spoke to the packed church in Philadelphia on May 26, 1826.

Boyhood friends in his Cherokee tribe called him Ga-la-gi-nah, or "buck deer," and some whites knew him as Buck Watie. Though his mother was of English descent, his father's Cherokee blood made him an Indian to Georgians.

It was Moravian missionaries who had helped him to dream of bringing peace and prosperity to all Cherokees. In order to do this, he needed a white man's education, which he received in Cornwall, Connecticut at a small missionary school.

General Elias Boudinot, a wealthy congressman and veteran of the American Revolution, was a patron of the school. He was pleased when the idealistic young Cherokee asked permission to adopt his name.

No longer Buck Watie, Elias Boudinot the younger won

Elias Boudinot (previously Buck Watie).

the hand of Harriet Ruggles Gold, but in the tiny village where he was studying, the interracial marriage had created such a furor that the school was forced to close. The money collected during the speaking tour went to Boston, where the alphabet devised by the Cherokee tribesman Sequoyah was cast into type to produce the first American Indian newspaper.

Young Boudinot was confronted by a dilemma. Under the patronage of the wealthy politician whose name he had taken, he could go to Washington to try to influence legislation favoring the Indians. Half white himself and having a lovely white wife, he would have no difficulty being accepted in the nation's capital. It would be an exciting and comfortable life. On the other hand, he could return to Georgia, live as a Cherokee, and face the hardships linked with that life.

Elias and Harriet agreed that he must go home and do what he could to help fellow tribesmen. He chose to edit a Cherokee newspaper at a salary of $300 a year, paid by missionary agencies.

The Cherokee nation had created a capital at the junction of the Coosawattee and Conasauga rivers, near present-day Calhoun, Georgia, so New Echota was the logical place from which to issue the newspaper that later gained fame as the *Cherokee Phoenix*.

Elias Boudinot printed the first issue of about 200 copies on February 21, 1828, with the stated purpose of bringing the white man's ways to the Cherokees, with peace as a by-product. However, instead of reducing strife, the *Phoenix* raised new tensions. Now that Indians could read editorials and news stories in their own language, white Georgians felt they presented new threats to them. Elias Boudinot and his printing press, and everything linked with it, would have to go.

However, peace-seeker Boudinot naively believed in the effectiveness of the white man's pacts, treaties, and legal agreements. Hence he assisted in drafting proposals that led to the agreement that the Cherokees would give up their Georgia land in return for cash and land in the distant west. To Boudinot, the treaty seemed to be the only hope for his nation. Although many tribesmen opposed it, he signed the document, believing it would prevent war.

Many months later, after the horrors of the "Trail of Tears" and the bitter disappointment of the "worthless" land in the Oklahoma Territory, Elias Boudinot died under the battle axes of his enraged fellow Cherokees. In June of 1839 came the end for this product of two opposing cultures who had renounced a pleasant life as a white man in the nation's capital to try to bring peace and permanency to the lives of his Indian relatives.

PART SIX:

The Fire of Genius

Wilbur G. Kurtz.

32

Wilbur Kurtz Came and Saw, and Atlanta Conquered

Wilbur George Kurtz, age twenty-one, gazed silently at his host, awestruck at finally being in the presence of a hero.

Captain William Fuller, conductor of the train stolen by Andrew's Raiders during the Civil War, had pursued and captured the locomotive *General*—part of the time using a second locomotive running backward at more than sixty miles an hour. Now he was pleased that a bright young artist from Chicago wanted a firsthand account of the adventure.

Kurtz made this trip to Atlanta in 1903 to confirm and amplify things he'd read. It was one of the nation's great adventure stories, he said. His judgment would later be confirmed by Walt Disney, who used it as the basis for his movie *The Great Locomotive Chase*.

During long conversations with Fuller, the Illinois native couldn't keep his eyes off the conductor's pretty and vivacious daughter Annie Laurie. Her influence helped to trigger revision of Julius Caesar's saying, "I came, I saw, I conquered." Wilbur Kurtz came from the city of Carl Sandburg, saw Atlanta . . . and was conquered. Moving to Atlanta in 1911, he soon married Annie Laurie Fuller and spent the next fifty-six years depicting the city as no one else has ever done.

For decades, everyone who knew Atlanta's past had realized that Whitehall Street was once the heart of the city. But what did it look like at the outbreak of the Civil War?

There were few photographs, but Atlantans had vivid memories. Some insisted that the Atlanta Hotel was the most important building of the time. Erected in 1846 by the Georgia Railroad, it was Atlanta's first brick building.

"But don't overlook the office of the *Intelligencer*, the leading daily newspaper of the era," others insisted. Kurtz interviewed scores of people, painstaking in his quest for specifics. He talked with those who had spent hours with locomotives in the 1860s and made meticulous notes. He jotted down dimensions of the Macon & Western Railroad depot, adjoining the *Intelligencer* office. He compiled records of the Trout House hotel and asked questions about the Masonic Building that once stood behind the hotel.

Wilbur Kurtz wasn't satisfied until he knew the size and color of bricks, the way a wagon was sprung, and the height

Surrender of Atlanta *by Wilbur G. Kurtz.*

of a lamp post. Combining hundreds of details from dozens of interviews, he painted "Whitehall Street Crossing, Atlanta, 1860."

The same precision went into an election day scene. When voters chose their first mayor on Saturday, January 29, 1848, there was just one polling place—Thomas Kile's grocery at a site close to present-day Five Points. When Kurtz depicted it, he included a capped chimney of a type not seen in the city for decades before his 1949 masterpiece was completed.

For posterity he preserved a vital scene in the drama of Atlanta's history. When General John B. Hood's Confederate army pulled out overnight, there were no military leaders to surrender to General William T. Sherman. Atlanta Mayor Calhoun and a few aides rode out on horseback to turn the city over to the victorious Yankees.

Although Sherman's photographer, George Barnard, had filmed many 1864 scenes, he was not present at the surrender ceremony. So artist Kurtz spent weeks researching details, then executed an eye-catching sketch of the drama.

The Illinois native left the city that "conquered" him a rare legacy of art. It was Kurtz who supervised restoration of the Cyclorama in 1934–36. Then he devoted his capacity for painstaking detail to the filming of *Gone With the Wind* in Hollywood. For instance, in the famous burning of Atlanta scene, it was he who prescribed that the blazing boxcars bear correct Union military markings.

The state of Georgia commissioned him to paint the murals for the Century of Progress Exposition in Chicago. In a city where for generations the term *Damnyankee* was one word, this northerner early on won a special niche. Atlanta will always be grateful to Wilbur Kurtz for his capturing and preservation of its past.

33

William Scarbrough Sent First Steamer Across the Atlantic

"November 30, 5:00 A.M. Saw Tybee light bearing WSW 4 leagues distant. Furled sails. On the flood tide, got under way with steam. Went up and anchored off the town."

That 1819 entry in the log book of Captain Moses Rogers sounds routine in the Space Age. When penned, it was a terse statement of triumph. Until that morning, Rogers had not seen the Tybee light for 192 days. There were times when he was not sure his S.S. *Savannah* would make it back to her home port.

Built at Corlear's Hook, New York, the sleek 380-ton vessel was designed to cross the Atlantic and to show the world that the great age of sail was about to come to an end. However, since her owner, William Scarbrough of Savannah had borrowed heavily to finance construction, he was careful to hedge his bets. He had his splendid vessel—of classical sailing-ship design—equipped with standard sails and rigging as well as with a steam engine and paddle wheels.

Noted political leader Joseph Habersham put up part of the $50,000 that went into the gamble to be first to cross the Atlantic with steam. Earlier, in 1817, Habersham had been a passenger on the maiden voyage of the coastal steamer *Charleston*, named for the port to which she went back and forth from Savannah.

Only a decade before that, Robert Fulton's *Clermont* had

been greeted with shouts of ridicule. Now steamers were well established in America's vital river trade, and a few specialized in short runs through coastal waters.

Savannah's key role in the huge and growing cotton trade had pushed her to sixteenth place in size among American cities. Several of her brokers and businessmen deserved the widely used title bestowed upon them: "Merchant Prince."

One such entrepreneur, William Scarbrough, admitted that steam engines had been used only for short voyages, but he was sure they could conquer the seas as well. Once he financed and built the *Savannah*, he planned to send her to England with a full load of passengers.

Because excursions on the Savannah River attracted eager participants, Scarbrough believed people were ready for transoceanic propulsion by steam engines. Even President James Monroe, who took a voyage on the river, pronounced the newfangled kind of travel to be "fast, and much smoother than anyone could have expected." Yet no one signed to go on the ship's maiden voyage and all thirty-two staterooms sailed empty.

S. S. Savannah used steam engine plus sails.

Entrepreneur William Scarbrough.

Still, James Monroe was a booster. As house guest of William Scarbrough, he issued a formal statement saying that America's prestige would receive a tremendous boost if her builders and seamen could show the world that steamers were suitable for use on the open seas.

On May 22, 1819, the *Savannah* steamed out of the port whose name she bore and then the Tybee light dropped below the horizon.

Today, after more than 150 years, carping critics point out that the experimental ship used sails for most of her Atlantic crossing, with Captain Rogers only firing up the boiler when he came close to land. At that time seamen of the British cruiser *Kite* mistook her for a ship on fire and chased the *Savannah* for a whole day off the coast of Ireland.

After twenty-seven days at sea, the *Savannah* puffed into Liverpool, creating an international sensation. Then the Georgia ship steamed proudly to Russia where Czar Alexander I presented Captain Rogers with an iron bench, which he brought back across the Atlantic and placed on display in Savannah's Owens-Thomas house.

The *Savannah* had proved what she could do. However, she was too small for heavy cargo, so the epoch-making vessel was stripped of her boiler and paddle wheels for reconversion into a sailing vessel. During an 1821 gale, she went down off Long Island.

Her life in the limelight was short, and her use of steam on the open seas was sporadic. But the impact of William Scarbrough's ship was so great that the anniversary of her sailing, May 22, became our National Maritime Day.

34

Laughing Gas Becomes Serious Stuff

"You are not afraid, are you?" inquired Crawford W. Long, M.D.

"A little, I guess," confessed James Venable. "It's not the gas. I've had enough of it to be a bit fond of it. But I'm not sure that I want a knife used on my neck, even after I pass out."

Venable, a student at tiny Jefferson Academy, had been troubled by cystic tumors since childhood. He called them wens and wanted them off, because they sometimes became sore. Only a surgeon's scalpel could remove them, and he feared the knife.

Finally Dr. Long persuaded him to sit for the operation to be performed in the physician's office, in Jefferson, the county seat of Jackson County.

Born in Danielsville, Crawford Long had studied in Athens and Lexington, Kentucky, before earning his M.D. in Philadelphia. There the Georgian and his fellow students had experimented with drugs that altered consciousness. Nitrous oxide was especially potent. Many young adults tried its effects, becoming hysterical with laughter, so it came to be called "laughing gas." Ether was also great party stuff.

In February, 1842, as a doctor in Georgia, Long had written to a supplier in nearby Athens, "I am entirely out of

Ether and wish some by tomorrow night. We have some girls in Jefferson who are anxious to see it taken."

During the next month, he reflected on "its exhilarating effects." Some of the young men who inhaled the potent stuff woke up to discover themselves bruised from falls they had not felt. Long believed if persons who sniffed it for a frolic were rendered insensible to pain, perhaps it could be put to more serious use.

Young James Venable's fear of pain presented a special opportunity to test Long's half-formed theory. "Pretend you're at a party," the physician suggested on March 30, 1842. "While you're having fun, I'll get one of those growths off your neck, and you'll never know it's gone until you wake up."

Though he was familiar with the effects of ether, Venable was hesitant. In the end, he agreed because he couldn't move his head without being aware of tumors that seemed to be growing larger.

That night in the little building that Crawford Long called his "shop," the first recorded surgery with anesthesia was performed. Andrew Thurmond, Venable's fellow student at the town academy, was the only witness. When it was over the surgeon billed his patient two dollars for the operation,

Dr. Crawford W. Long.

plus twenty-five cents for the ether. A few weeks later Venable had his second tumor removed for the same price.

Residents of the village and nearby farm families had other painless operations performed in succeeding months. Even amputation of a toe and two fingers went smoothly, with no suffering during the surgery, the patient reported.

However, the young physician did not publish his discovery to the medical profession.

Up East, there was an entirely different reaction.

In 1844 dentist Horace Wells used nitrous oxide on himself while having a tooth pulled. In 1846 Dr. William T. G. Morton, at the recommendation of Boston chemist Charles Jackson, used ether during surgery. Publicity given these medical sensations prompted Dr. Long in faraway Georgia to put the story of his own pioneer work into print.

However, outside the deep South, hardly anyone read Long's account. The competing claims of Morton, Jackson, and Wells had the medical world's attention.

Eventually Dr. Crawford W. Long left the village where medical history was made, practicing briefly in Atlanta and settling permanently in Athens. There he built up a fine surgical practice and lived in comfort but not affluence. At his death in June, 1878, he was unknown outside his native state.

Decades passed. Researchers began probing more deeply into the story of one of modern medicine's greatest breakthroughs. Claims of the three northern men who had been hailed as "the fathers of surgical anesthesia" were carefully investigated and it was discovered that their experiments had been launched a full two years after Crawford Long had used his scalpel upon a youth who had a pain in the neck.

Today the family doctor born in Danielsville is commemorated by a statue in his home town. A great hospital in Atlanta bears his name. So does a county of 403 square miles, and the family doctor from Jefferson is revered in medical centers everywhere.

35

Heisman Guided Yellow Jackets to All-Time Record

Georgia Tech's Golden Tornadoes fared badly during the 1903–04 football season, so college leaders decided to take a bold step and hire a full-time coach.

Ohio-born John Heisman hadn't stayed anywhere very long. He began coaching football at Oberlin where in 1892 he turned out a team with a perfect seven-game record for the season. From Oberlin he went to Akron, then to Auburn, and to Clemson in 1900.

Heisman's salary at Clemson was so low that he became a Shakespearean actor during off-season, and Tech got him by offering him a salary boost of fifty dollars a month.

Critics called him eccentric, but admirers insisted that he was a lopsided genius who might have been right in forbidding his players to use hot water and soap during the week. "The stuff is debilitating," said Heisman in the exaggerated stage voice he nearly always used, a carryover from his moonlighting as an actor.

Although his Golden Tornadoes didn't win a game in 1912, by 1914 Heisman had transformed them into the Yellow Jackets, whom he led to the Southern championship. For three successive years they remained on top. In one period they played a string of thirty games without a single loss.

Concerned for the safety of his players, the coach led a

successful crusade against use of the flying wedge. "The human frame just isn't equal to the wedge," he said. "Use your brain instead of your body whenever you can."

That principle led him to an innovation. Studying rule books, he concluded they didn't prohibit concealment of the ball. So he developed and used the hidden-ball play.

His "Heisman shift," brought out very early, involved having the entire team, except the center, drop behind the scrimmage line. Backs lined up at right angles to the rush line. Awed sports writer George Trevor described the maneuver for the *New York Sun* newspaper: "At the shift signal, the phalanx deployed with the suddenness of a Jeb Stuart cavalry raid, catching the defense off balance."

Along with the famous Heisman shift, the Tech coach decided to put everything he had into a 1916 game. He'd been challenged by assistant coach Bill Alexander, who said that "If we don't beat Cumberland by fifty points, we ought to lose."

Yellow Jacket Coach John Heisman.

Halfback Everett ("Strup") Strupper broke into the conversation between coaches. "If we score 100 will you set 'em up for the gang, Alex?"

"Nope," Alexander responded. "But if you make 200 points, I'll set up the varsity, the scrub, and the frosh."

That was all Heisman and his fire-eating squad needed. Drawn from a student body of 843, the Yellow Jackets didn't have a significant numerical edge. Cumberland, with more than 500 students, had won the All-Southern championship in 1907, and remained a powerful opponent.

Preparing for the big game, Tech's coach cut the water allowance for his players. In typical Heisman style, he demanded that members of the squad eat their meat nearly raw.

Playing before a crowd of less than one thousand spectators who stood because there were no bleachers, Tech made twenty first downs to Cumberland's none. Tech gained 501 net yards rushing to Cumberland's –42. Not counting kick-off returns, the Yellow Jackets moved the ball 959 yards. Cumberland had a net loss of 28 yards for the game.

It was strictly ground action—pure old-fashioned bone-crushing football. Not a pass was thrown.

Six plays into the third quarter, a conversion made the score Tech 154, Cumberland 0. That broke the 1912 world record of 153 points, scored by Michigan.

"Our crew of eleven worked like a mowing machine eating its way through a field of ripe grain," said the jubilant coach. Yet even the man whose name later became attached to the most coveted of all college football trophies consented to stop the carnage

As recalled by Tech's Dean Griffin, "Officials decided to call the game after 7½ minutes into the fourth quarter. If they hadn't done that, the score would have gone past 300." As it was, the final whistle blew when it stood 222–0. Today, Heisman's masterpiece game rates a full paragraph in many editions of the *Guinness Book of World Records*.

Rule changes make chances of a repeat performance of the 1916 debacle just about nil, so the record score is apt to remain tops in college football for a long time.

When Heisman and his wife separated soon after the big win, they tossed coins to decide who'd stay in Atlanta. She won. That sent the coach to New York City near the tail end of his career, where he worked as athletic director for the wealthy, but not-so-athletic, Downtown Athletic Club.

In 1935 well-heeled members of the club put up the money to create a trophy in the form of a two-foot bronze runner who is stiff-arming a tackle. Naturally, they called it the Downtown Athletic Club Trophy.

Before the trophy was awarded for the first time, John W. Heisman died and admirers managed to get his name attached to the award. That is how a Tech coach who wasn't altogether certain he shouldn't have been a Shakespearean actor won a kind of immortality that is afforded to very few.

222-0 game was played on field where spectators stood on sidelines to watch.

36

"Blind Tom" Bethune Awed Crowned Heads of Europe

Who was Thomas Gage Bethune? Precisely *what* was he?

Contemporaries thought they knew the answer to both questions. In the United States, Britain, and France they flocked to hear the musical prodigy perform. After having applauded wildly, they called him "idiot" and "a little nigger boy who's a freak of nature."

Bethune's life story is better known now than it was a century ago. Born and reared in slavery, before he died he was credited with having attracted "more people to see and hear him than any other living wonder."

Idiot, he clearly was not. Given a different set of circumstances, he might have become a great composer.

Born on May 25, 1849, in Muscogee County, Tom belonged to James N. Bethune, a plantation owner and ardent secessionist who was usually called Colonel or General. To him the infant slave was a liability because he was blind.

Today, he'd be called "legally blind," since his vision was limited to light perception plus recognition of familiar persons and objects at close range. When he took to the concert stage, he was labeled "completely blind." His manager realized very early that a blind performer would stir up much more interest than an equally versatile one with vision, however limited.

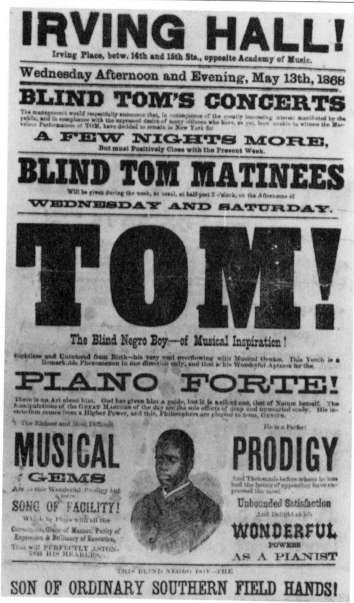

IRVING HALL!

Irving Place, betw. 14th and 15th Sts., opposite Academy of Music.

Wednesday Afternoon and Evening, May 13th, 1868

BLIND TOM'S CONCERTS

The management would respectfully announce that, in consequence of the greatly increasing interest manifested by the public, and in compliance with the expressed desire of many citizens who have, as yet, been unable to witness the Marvelous Performances of TOM, have decided to remain in New York for

A FEW NIGHTS MORE,

But must Positively Close with the Present Week.

BLIND TOM MATINEES

Will be given during the week, as usual, at half-past 2 o'clock, on the Afternoons of

WEDNESDAY AND SATURDAY.

TOM!

The Blind Negro Boy—of Musical Inspiration!

Sightless and Untutored from Birth—his very soul overflowing with Musical Genius. This Youth is a Remarkable Phenomenon in one direction only, and that is his Wonderful Aptness for the

PIANO FORTE!

There is no Art about him. God has given him a guide, but it is a silent one, that of Nature herself. The manipulations of the GREAT MASTERS of the day are the sole efforts of deep and unwearied study. His instruction comes from a Higher Power, and this, Philosophers are pleased to term, GENIUS.

The Richest and Most Difficult   He is a Perfect

MUSICAL GEMS

Are in this Wonderful Prodigy but here

SONG OF FACILITY!

Which he Plays with all the Correctness, Grace of Manner, Purity of Expression & Brilliancy of Execution, That will PERFECTLY ASTONISH HIS HEARERS.

PRODIGY

And Thousands before whom he has had the honor of appearing have expressed the most

Unbounded Satisfaction

And Delight at his

WONDERFUL POWERS

AS A PIANIST

THIS BLIND NEGRO BOY—THE

SON OF ORDINARY SOUTHERN FIELD HANDS!

Following the custom of using surnames of owners, the boy was called Thomas Gage Bethune. His fascination with sounds of all kinds was noticed very early. Still, he created a stir one night. Creeping into his master's mansion, he began to play on the newly acquired piano a melody he had heard for the first time only a few hours earlier.

No one in the big house knew what to make of Tom's unplanned demonstration. Totally without schooling, he couldn't even repeat the alphabet. No one had given him any instruction in music, yet his deft touch and sure sense of rhythm announced him as a master musician.

The astonished Colonel Bethune took his slave to a German music teacher in Columbus, the county seat. "No, sir, I can't teach him anything," the musician said after having heard the boy perform. "Just let him hear fine playing. He'll work it out by himself after a while, regardless, but he'll do it sooner by hearing fine music."

Music stores in Columbus ordered a wide range of popular and classical compositions and local pianists played these for the growing boy. As predicted, he drank in melodies eagerly. Soon he demonstrated that he could memorize every note while hearing a composition once.

By now, Colonel Bethune knew he had a money maker on his hands. He turned other interests over to relatives and began exhibiting the prodigy whom he billed as Blind Tom.

The emancipation of slaves had no significant effect on the relationship between the black prodigy and Colonel Bethune, who was his legal guardian. No one knows how much Colonel Bethune made from that relationship. Estimates of the musician's earnings range as high as $100,000 a year, at a time when Abraham Lincoln's salary as president was $25,000 a year.

Blind Tom gave triumphant performances in London, Paris, and most major cities of Western Europe, playing from a repertoire of more than 2,000 compositions. He often demonstrated his ability to reproduce perfectly a new composition, one twenty minutes in length, after one hearing.

As an adolescent he delighted and amazed audiences by playing two tunes simultaneously while singing a third. In Albany, New York, he once played "Yankee Doodle" in B flat with his right hand. With his left hand he played "Fisher's Hornpipe" in C. At the same time, he sang "Tramp, Tramp, Tramp" flawlessly, in still another key.

His career spanned a period of more than thirty years of sell-out performances, yet today, many scholars admit bewilderment that no one during his life gave him serious attention as a composer. He wrote "The Rain Storm" at age five, composed "The Battle of Manassas" as an interpretation of Civil War agonies, and at least seventy other original compositions have been catalogued. How many were lost without mention is unknown.

Georgia's first black to become an international celebrity is a bigger enigma today than during Civil War years. Had he been given the best of musical training rather than being exploited, what would Thomas Gage Bethune have accomplished?

Thomas Gage Bethune.

37

Agricultural Agent from Indiana Built Delta Air Lines

Lieutenant H. R. Harris of the brand-new Huff Da-land Dusting Corporation reached Macon on March 17, 1925. His Petrel 5 plane, powered by a 200-hp Wright E4 engine, made the 180-mile flight from Birmingham in just over two hours "without the slightest mishap."

Harris, heading a group of twelve pilots and fifteen me-chanics, eventually built up a fleet of eighteen especially equipped planes—nine for use, and nine for back-up. A hangar at old Camp Wheeler, five miles south of Macon, served as headquarters. From that center they conducted the world's first experiment in commercial use of airplanes for crop dusting.

Macon was selected for the start of a program that mushroomed beyond anyone's expectation because cotton fields and peach orchards surrounded it in middle and south Georgia. Also, farseeing Bibb County leaders, hoping to make the region an aviation center, agreed to spend $5,000 preparing a field usable in four directions, including one runway that was 1,800 feet long.

This radical new idea was the brain child of an agricul-tural agent, Indiana native C. E. Woolman. He had become enamored with aviation after taking his first flight as a small boy and had won a degree in agricultural engineering. Then he worked under the extension department of Louisiana

State University in early experiments aimed at control of the boll weevil.

Calcium arsenate, applied as a dust, looked promising. Yet the process of getting it into fields was tedious and costly. Woolman knew that planes had once been used to spray infested catalpa trees. Why not cotton?

Federal authorities, doubtful that the idea could be put to practical use, finally provided two army-owned DeHavilland DN–4s, for which Woolman and Dr. R. B. Coad designed dusting equipment. Progress was tediously slow—until fate took a hand.

When an Ogdensburg, New York, airplane executive was forced to land in the Louisiana delta, he learned of the crop dusting experiment. If it worked, he believed it could create a new market for his company's planes. So he created a new division, the Huff Daland, with Woolman serving as vice-president and field manager.

Crop-dusters used in Peru bore a llama as insignia.

In charge of the Macon experiment, Woolman charged farmers seven dollars per acre for five dustings. New equipment, especially produced, provided a uniform spray and the Macon *Daily Telegraph* reported that a plane could cover twelve acres per minute of flying time. However, it was costly to maintain a fleet of planes for brief seasonal use. Therefore the innovative Woolman conceived the idea of doing the same thing in South America where the seasons are reversed below the equator. He shipped planes to Peru by steamer, and dusted so successfully in 1926 that work expanded to seven immense Peruvian valleys.

Peruvian distances, plus the rugged Andean terrain, triggered for Woolman a spin-off idea. Why not use planes to transport mail?

Germans who had arrived at the same idea were seeking a Peruvian franchise. Against stiff competition, the American won rights to become the first airline operator south of the equator in the western hemisphere. He inaugurated a fifteen-hundred-mile route from Peru to Ecuador in 1927.

Suddenly the Huff Daland organization faced financial problems. Reverses by the parent corporation led officials to place the company on the market.

Woolman found backing in Monroe, Louisiana, and purchased all Huff Daland equipment, forming the operating fleet of a new corporation named for the Mississippi delta where its headquarters were then located. Newly formed Delta Air Lines continued crop dusting, but also carried mail and passengers.

Expanding many times and moving its corporate headquarters to Atlanta in 1941, Delta has become one of the world's biggest air lines. Crop dusting was discontinued in 1966.

Still, C. E. Woolman's Macon start is far from forgotten. Delta employees bought a vintage Huff Daland duster in 1968, restored it, and presented it to the Smithsonian Institution as a memorial to the genius of Delta's founder.

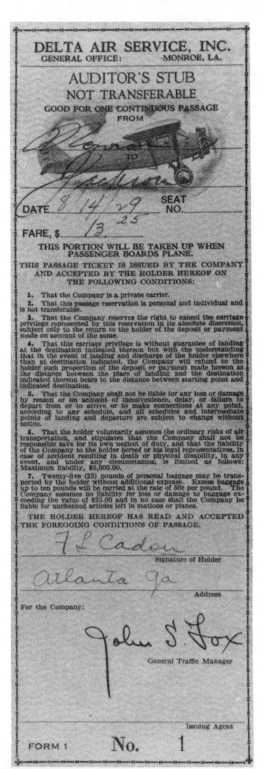

Delta's first passenger ticket, August 4, 1929, provided for flight from Monroe, Louisiana, to Jackson, Louisiana, for $13.25.
COURTESY OF DELTA AIR LINES

38

To Beat the Law, Doc Pemberton
Stirred Up a Substitute

Atlanta's Asa G. Candler, who made Coca-Cola the world's most widely consumed carbonated beverage, was a staunch churchman of the Methodist variety. A century ago, that meant he was also an ardent prohibitionist.

Prohibitionist Candler and his successors in the Coca-Cola empire have had good reason to thank voters who counted themselves "dry," for it was activity on the part of anti-alcohol forces that stirred an already creative businessman into a burst of activity.

John S. Pemberton, a native of Knoxville, Georgia, was a pharmacist and wholesale druggist in Columbus whose thriving business was interrupted by the Civil War. During the war he led Pemberton's Cavalry, serving for a time under Georgia's General Joseph Wheeler.

A few years after Appomattox, Pemberton moved to Atlanta. There he made and sold Indian Queen Hair Dye, Globe of Flower Cough Syrup, Triplex Liver Pills, and a host of other medications.

One of his best sellers was French Wine Coca. Doc, as everyone called him, advertised it as "a Delightful Nerve Tonic and Stimulant that Never Intoxicates." It proved so popular that he registered it as a trademark in 1885.

Experts believe that Pemberton's nostrum included an extract from South America's "sacred herb,"—the coca plant.

Doc Pemberton, wholesale druggist.

Peruvian coca was considered to have marvelous effects; those who consumed it were believed to be able to accomplish astonishing physical feats, without fatigue.

How much coca was in Pemberton's recipe is unknown.

Wine was another matter, and Pemberton used it freely to appeal to men whose wives didn't permit use of alcohol, but who approved use of patent medicines.

According to Doc, his French Wine Coca was also fortified with kola nut extract. Whatever it included, the beverage seemed to be headed toward the top of the sales chart. His chemical plant, built at a cost of $160,000 was very profitable.

Then in 1885 voters of Fulton County voted dry by a margin of 228 votes in a local option referendum. Every saloon had to close its doors on July 1, 1886.

Many a merchant in Doc's position would have tried to find a buyer for the chemical plant. Instead of doing so, he got busy; challenge fired his creative genius.

The story goes that he installed a three-legged iron pot in his back yard. Stirring and tasting behind his house, adding new ingredients and stirring again, he produced a formula to replace outlawed French Wine Coca. Since the new mixture included coca from South America plus kola from Africa, Doc called the new mixture Coca-Cola.

Willis E. Venable managed the biggest soda fountain in Atlanta, in Jacob's Pharmacy at the corner of Peachtree and Marietta Streets. There the first Coca-Cola was served to a customer on Saturday, May 8, 1886.

It was marketed originally as the "Ideal Brain Tonic" and reliever of fatigue. So labeled, Coca-Cola didn't have many devotees during early years, but the slow sales presented an opportunity to Asa G. Candler. In a series of complicated purchases that were completed in 1891, he bought all rights to Coca-Cola for $2,300. Knowing he had to boost sales, he plowed all revenue from the drink into advertising.

Soon Candler, who had been a wholesale druggist selling Delectalave A Dentifrice, Botanic Blood Balm, and other proprietary medicines, dropped them altogether, gambled at least $50,000 on the future of Coca-Cola, and incorporated the company in 1892. A year later, he registered the famous trademark. Ever since sales of the secret-formula drink created by Doc Pemberton's response to prohibition have never stopped growing at exponential rates.

Marketing genius Asa G. Candler.

Index

Boldface signifies an illustration.